Mike's

MICHAEL SHEEHAN

Michael Sheehan was born and raised in St. Paul, graduating from the University of Minnesota in 1962. He spent 35 years as a "utility writer", producing feature articles, speech and AV scripts, advertising copy and PR programs for a variety of clients. During that period he served as PR Supervisor for a major utility, publisher of small tabloid newspapers, ad-agency owner, and VP-Communications for the Better Business Bureau of Southern Arizona. *Dogs in the Hot Moon*, cataloging a single chapter in the life of his great-grandfather, is his first novel. Following residences in Colorado and southern California, he moved to Tucson, Arizona in 1979. He and his wife Carole have recently completed building a straw bale home near the Grand Canyon, where they now reside.

Printed in the
United States of America
for
Inspired Originals Publishing House
Munds Park, Arizona
U.S.A.

1st Edition May 28, 2011

Copyright © 2011 "Dogs in The Hot Moon"

LCCN: 2011909058

Credit is given for the photograph of Timothy J. Sheehan to Joel Emmons Whitney, Minnesota Historical Society
Credit for the Drawing of Dakota attacking a camp, 1862 is given to Martin's Gallery, Minnesota Historical Society

Dedicated to
Patty Dame, niece and family historian,
whose interest ignited my own,
and to Carole Sheehan,
who waited patiently
while I tended the fire.

DOGS IN THE HOT MOON
T.J. Sheehan and the Sioux Uprising of 1862
by
Michael Sheehan

Major General Winfield Scott
General-In-Chief, U.S.A.
I need hardly say to you, sir, well acquainted as you are with the strength of the different Indian tribes of the west, that the Sioux or Dakotas are the most powerful and warlike tribe on the continent.
                        Henry H. Sibley
                        Letter promoting the
                        establishment of Ft. Ridgely,
                        Minnesota, July 12, 1852

You will die like rabbits when the hungry wolves hunt them in the Hard Moon.
                        Taoyateduta (Little Crow)
                        Speech to braves prior to uprising
                        August 18, 1862

It appeared to me that the gates of hell were broken open and all the firy (sic) dragons of its bottomless pits were approaching.
                        Lt. Timothy J. Sheehan
                        Personal journal
                        August 22, 1862

PROLOGUE

August 18, 1862

"Lieutenant! They're coming!"

The compound churned, its occupants outnumbered by the streams of panicked settlers. Careening wagons and screaming survivors rended the early Fall mist. Blue-uniformed Union troops sliced through the gray haze, corralling wide-eyed horseflesh, tending the wounded, quieting the hysterical, and commandeering doors, desks, bales and any other solid object that might provide cover in this fort-without-walls.

Timothy J. Sheehan, 26-year-old 1st Lieutenant, 5th Minnesota Volunteers, clambered up the rickety ladder to the roof of the fort's tack shed and snatched the bulky field-glasses from the young lookout. Annoyed at both the fear evident in the boy's outcry and his own response to it, he already knew what he would see.

He wiped the drizzle from the lenses and drew them to his eyes, bringing into focus the objects of his dread. For moments he watched, fascinated. The red bastards, barely visible through the August mist, were right there. This really was happening.

Captain Marsh had rushed off chasing "a few outlaws". These were no outlaws. It looked like the whole Sioux nation was on the march, the western horizon filled by a writhing caravan of garishly painted warriors, flanked by a string of buckboards and hay wagons awkwardly propelled by women of the tribe hauling cargoes of child-warriors waving switches and jumping up and down as if on some sort of gruesome lark. A handful of the real warriors, mounted, were careening back and forth along the caravan, thrusting their weapons and engaging one another in mock battle.

Two were unseated from their mounts while Sheehan watched. Where the hell did they get all those horses?

"Whupping up the troops they are, Lieutenant. Ain't a one of 'em come by them buckboards peaceful". Master Sergeant Harry Kennedy, having mounted the rickety perch unnoticed, growled his opinion between streams of tobacco juice propelled with barely an error through a crack in the shed's roof.

"They're purloined, Sergeant, wrested from the slaughtered to carry off the booty of the next to be slaughtered", Sheehan replied, projecting a calm he did not feel.

"Presumptuous of the vermin, I'd say", Kennedy responded. "And stupid. The stupidest thing I ever seen growed men do. It's gonna backfire *bad*. Whatever they thought was wrong's gonna seem like corn pie compared to what they're buyin' here. God, let me be here to see it."

Sheehan heard only snatches of his sergeant's rant, reliving the sights he and his troop had encountered on their forced march back to Fort Ridgely less than a half-day earlier. 42 miles in barely over nine hours, straight into the gates of hell. Terrorized, incoherent settlers stretching beyond view, fleeing eastward past the protection of the fort itself, thinking distance alone would bring protection from the marauding bands of Dakota from the Yellow River agency. Men with gaping wounds. Ashen-faced children with torn limbs. Pregnant women, bellies pin-cushioned with arrows.

Jaw muscles twitching, his composure renewed with his mounting sense of outrage, the young officer spat as well, glanced once more at the invading horde, and returned the glasses to the now silent lookout.

"Good sight, son", he said. "What do you figure, Sergeant?"

"'Bout two miles, Lieutenant. It almost don't look like they're coming here, but if they turn, and don't speed up none, we'll have company in about an hour", Kennedy mused. "If they decide to lope them scraggly old horses - about twenty minutes. What first, Lieutenant?"

Sheehan looked up at the beefy, florid-faced Irishman, his inferior in formal rank only, a fact cordially accepted by both men. "You need *instructions* now, do you?", he asked.

"Only if you know something I don't", Kennedy replied. "If not, if you might be so kind as to direct the civilians, I'll get my boys in their proper positions. By God it's going to be a turkey shoot, sir".

With no response forthcoming, Kennedy clambered down from the narrow rooftop, taking the young lookout with him as aide and courier. Sheehan stayed, eyeing the western horizon, cursing the rain, hoping that the horde might divert to the village of New Ulm with its easier civilian pickings. But even without field glasses, he could see that the southern-most tip of the warrior column was angling toward the fort. He turned to survey the resources he had to line up against them, and felt his stomach tighten at the chaos below. This was not the rebellion he had signed on to fight.

CHAPTER ONE

May 15, 1861

Whereas the laws of the United States have been for some time past and are now opposed, and the execution thereof obstructed in the states of South Carolina, Georgia, Alabama, Florida, Mississippi, Louisiana and Texas, by combinations too powerful to be suppressed by the ordinary course of judicial proceedings, or by the powers vested in the marshals by law

Now, therefore, I, Abraham Lincoln, President of the United States, in virtue of the power in me vested by the Constitution and the laws, have thought fit to call forth, and hereby do call forth the militia of the several States of the Union, in the aggregate number of seventy-five thousand, in order to suppress said combinations, and to cause the laws to be duly executed.

The details for this object will be immediately communicated to the State authorities through the War Department.

I appeal to all loyal citizens to favor, facilitate, and aid this effort to maintain the honor, the integrity, and the existence of our National Union, and the perpetuity of popular government, and to redress wrongs already long enough endured.

I deem it proper to say that the first service assigned to the forces hereby called forth will probably be to repossess the forts, places and property which have been seized from the Union, and in every event the utmost care will be observed, consistently with the objects aforesaid, to avoid any devastation, any destruction of or interference with property, or any disturbance of peaceful citizens in any part of the country.

And I hereby command the persons composing the combinations aforesaid to disperse and retire peacefully to their respective abodes within twenty days from date.

Deeming that the present condition of public affairs presents an extraordinary occasion, I do hereby, in virtue of the power in me vested by the Constitution, convene both Houses of Congress. Senators and Representatives are therefore summoned to assemble at their respective chambers at twelve o'clock noon, on Thursday, the fourth day of July next, then and there to consider and determine which measures as, in their wisdom, the public safety and interest may seem to demand.

In Witness, etc, Abraham Lincoln.
By the President. May 3, 1861

The notice, a wrinkled and grimy hand-printed parchment sheet, was delivered by a surly and exhausted rider aboard a dun mare so overridden her sweat had turned to foam. As town clerk of the village of Albert Lea, Minnesota, Tim Sheehan was first to view it. Even before he'd finished reading, the clamor surrounding the courier's arrival brought the sleepy village alive, and put the young Irish immigrant in the position of stage manager as he pushed the document onto the pair of horseshoe nails protruding from the porch wall of the clerk's office. He relayed the main message of the announcement to the gathering throng, and stepped back.

"What was that, Tim?" Sheehan squinted up at Esau Weaver, town farrier and a full head taller than himself, shielded his eyes from the sun and said simply, "War, Esau. We're going to war."

"Huh! You mean *you're* going to war", Esau replied, shaking his head. "I've got a wife and two kids, and if a bunch of rummies a thousand miles away want to own a darkie, and the darkie don't take care of himself, why should I?"

Sheehan looked up. "Because we may not have a choice", he said.

News of the southerners' rebellion, and the firing on Ft. Sumter, had reached the village of Albert Lea a week earlier, passed on by a circuit rider from the office of Minnesota governor Alexander Ramsey. It was not unexpected, and had been received quietly, and somberly, like the death of a distant relative. Even the Hayes twins, 13-year-old roughhousing kids given to pranks and party jokes, were subdued in their response to this new appeal. News of an uprising a two-week march away over an issue no one here could understand failed to trigger panic among these pioneers. This was someone else's battle. There were implements to be fixed, fields to be plowed, clothes to be sewn, reading and writing to be taught.

But the courier's announcement, direct from the hand of the President of the United States, gouged deep into the veneer of just-another-day calm. The President had said it *was* their battle. No guns could be heard, no greycoats with slashing sabers rode through their town, but everyone knew the war was real. Hundreds of Union troops had already been killed, it was said - even if not *here*.

CHAPTER TWO

The reality of the situation and its likely impact on the settlers of Albert Lea festered for the next many weeks as the summer wore on, and the crops were nurtured, and ultimately harvested.. "Wait and see" grew to an overriding philosophy as the community weighed the needs of the nation against those closer to home.

October 4, 1861

Sheehan scanned the crowd that had assembled before the clerk's office on this late Fall evening. The stark branches of the overhanging oaks, already stripped bare by chilled winds that foretold the early onset of winter, added to the gloomy nature of the meeting. Gatherings here were usually social events - a wedding, introduction of a new baby, the annual post-harvest hoedown. This was not, and the faces in the crowd reflected its gravity.

The war to date had not gone well for the Union. At Sewell's Point, the first real response to the attack on Ft. Sumter, Union gunboats and rebel artillery fought to a draw. The Union's attack on June 10 at Big Bethel had been rebuffed. Missouri's pro-confederate State Guard had defeated the state's pro-Union Home Guard on June 19. The rebels won at Carthage, Blackburn's Ford and Bull Run in July. Two victories and two losses in August. The Union Cavalry defeated by the Missouri State Guard on September 2. Union forces lost at Lexington after a week-long battle. A loss at the Battle of Liberty September 17. There were some minor victories and some inconclusive engagements, but overall, it wasn't good. The "south", to the alarm of many in the community, was no longer confined to the distant fields of Georgia and Virginia. Battles were taking place in *Missouri*, with only a single state serving as buffer to the peace the Minnesotans prized so dearly. The thing was getting closer to home.

With no elected mayor, longtime Sheriff Fred Ruble had been briefed by Sheehan, who appeared to be taking the war personally, and asked to handle the gathering. The crops were in; now the decisions. Ruble was respected by most in the community, a sturdy man, approaching 6 feet tall, given to impatience with the foolhardy, and known as a straight talker

"First off, the Union is under siege", he began. "What you've been hearing and reading is true. We're *not winning*. Hundreds of our boys are rotting in the ground down there. Maybe thousands by now. The rebels are on some sort of damnable mission. They plan to change how we think and how we live. They're not about to give up their damned slaves, and they're just plain mowing down anyone who disagrees with them. They're not 'negotiating'. They're shooting. They need to be stopped. *Somebody's* got to do it. If it isn't there it will have to be here. I'm for there. And we need to be part of seeing that it is".

The sheriff's response was too simple for many in the crowd, who responded with barely audible muttering and downcast glances.

Esau Weaver was first to speak up. "We *don't* need to be part of it, Sheriff. Those boys haven't tried to put *me* in chains, or anybody else around here as far as I can tell. We're talking about a bunch of Negroes made to work hard, and they're generally a pretty husky bunch who should be able to fare for themselves. It's not like they was being tortured or killed, and it's not our fight!"

Mary Ellen Madden, her husband hospitalized in St. Paul after being stomped by a draft horse, spoke for many of the women in the crowd. "Who you gonna take, Sheriff? How many? My man's been gone for three weeks and I can tell you it's no picnic running a plow with one at the breast, and four mouths to feed, and stuff breaking down left and right. Tad'll be back in a week but when will the ones you take be back? What happens when winter comes? Who'll take care of the families of those who *don't* come back?"

After several more in the crowd voiced their opinions, almost all negative, Sheriff Ruble took a step back on the porch and raised his hands in front of him, crossing them as if warding off a swarm of insects. He didn't know when the men would come back, he admitted, nor how much they would be paid, nor what would happen to the widows who would undoubtedly be created from this mess. This wasn't his idea. It wasn't Lincoln's either. He didn't fire on the south; the south just up and started killing Union soldiers and civilians, and were even now taking towns in the north, and if they weren't stopped that thousand-mile buffer that seemed so important way back when, and already hewn down to half that and less in some places, would be totally chewed up before you knew it.

"And you boys, and your women too", he said, "could be defending farms and families from your front porches, damnit".

It wasn't what was expected from the normally laconic sheriff.

Tim Sheehan stepped into the pause that followed Sheriff Ruble's animated response. The sheriff had served almost as a surrogate father to the then 19-year-old immigrant ever since he'd arrived in Albert Lea nearly five years earlier. The young clerk didn't like to see his friend challenged, civil though it might be, but felt his face flush for even deeper reasons.

"Hold on, now", he said as he rose from the porch bench and moved to stand by the sheriff. "We don't know how this thing is going to end. It might end by Friday - or five years from Friday. We don't know how many of the 75,000 Lincoln asked for need to come from Minnesota. There are a lot of states where the fighting is already going on. We don't *know*."

"And I need to say something for myself."

Members of the crowd who had begun to leave turned to hear the clerk's words. Sheehan had proven himself an honest, hardworking and popular town clerk, now building a cabin on his own 160 acre plot, and a man who generally spoke with both wit and reason.

"I doubt that prison wagons are going to raid our town in the dark of night and haul off any soul familiar with the inside of a trigger guard", he said."Our contingent will be called the Minnesota Volunteer Infantry. *Volunteer.* You'll go if you can, and want, not if you don't. So sleep well. I won't."

"I'm practically itchin' to go. This isn't about a bunch of rag-tags off on a killing spree. It's a bunch of *states* who want to be their own *country*, and in order to get there have to come right through here. Their name, their laws, their way of doing things, their version of 'honor', their colored servants on the ends of leashes. That OK with you, Esau?" Esau said nothing.

Sheehan paused and looked down at his boots, his hat obscuring the glistening in his eyes.

"Eleven years ago I arrived in New York after a miserable crossing aboard what they called a 'coffin ship'. A month escaping a famine that had already killed a million Irish souls, women and children, and driven another million out to *anywhere* else. You could see the ribs on most of us. It was a 90-foot boat; two decks; four honey pots, 350 men, women and children and nary a wall between any of us. They were called coffin ships because of the boxes they carried to slide off the new corpses that popped up every day from disease, and age, and starvation and seas that made you damn your own stomach. We left with 350, arrived with 33 less. 33 over the side. You got so you were glad to see 'em go; it gave you just that few inches more space.

"When we arrived in America we bent and kissed the ground - and got booted in the ass while we were down. The Irish were looked on as monkeys, and treated like it. In Europe we had to accept it. In America we didn't. We worked hard, the Chinese and us building railroads, and canals, and tanning leather, and doing what others wouldn't. And we were accepted. I farm a plot today nearly as big as my whole village in Ireland. I own my own horse, my own tools, my homestead. I've a good job, good friends, a woman I love. I found every one of these in the *United* States of America and I, for one, don't plan to see them busted up. I'm signing up, and I'd be proud to have any one of you join me."

A bit flustered by his own rhetoric, Sheehan stepped down from the porch to scattered applause, most, he noted, coming from the single men of the village - including the 13-year-old Hayes twins.

CHAPTER THREE

His words didn't mobilize the entire region, but they did get people to talking, and served as a public commitment for the young clerk himself. He knew where he had to go, and within days had wrapped up his affairs and - much to his surprise - had attracted some 14 young men from throughout the county willing to follow him to Ft. Snelling. Blacksmith Esau Weaver stood in the first rank.

October 11, 1861

Fort Snelling had become the central training depot for the area's recruits for the War of the Rebellion. It had been built 40 years earlier atop a bluff overlooking the confluence of the Mississippi and St. Peters (later Minnesota) Rivers. The nine-square-mile, 200,000-acre site had been acquired from the Sioux in 1805 through a treaty negotiated by Zebulon Pike on the orders of President Thomas Jefferson. The purchase was later valued at $2,000 by the United States Senate, a dime an acre. At the signing, the Indians received $200 in trinkets and 60 gallons of rum. Among the signers was Le Petit Corbeau, the grandfather of Little Crow.

The fort had long since outlived its intended purpose as the frontier surged beyond it, and three years back had been sold to a developer to plot into residential lots. With the opening of the war, the developer leased it back to the government.

It was early on a Sunday at the fort, just days after Sheehan's oration. He and Esau led a caravan of nine riders and four horse-drawn wagons, The weather was clear and brisk, mostly sunny but temperatures in the 40s and the ground still solid from the freezing temperatures of the night before.

It was a bare caravan, the recruits having been told that the only belongings they could keep were those that could be carried on their own backs. The wagons packed four passengers each, and rucksacks for three. The fourth in each wagon was along for the ride to the fort, then to return the wagon to Albert Lea. Two of the drivers were wives, one a brother, one a mature 9-year-old son who had been charged with protecting his mom during his dad's absence, and was anxious to do so.

The going was slow over the still rutted roadway. Even with an early start and continuing on past sunset it would take two full days to sight the fort, and a second night's camp to allow the group to enter the garrison in a fresh condition.

The trip proved uneventful, save for the creativity of the new recruits in their efforts to out-bravado one another. Good-natured taunts and boasts were the order of the day, and kept the caravan in a mood lighter than its purpose.

Camp stirred at daylight on the third day out, not out of eagerness so much as the discomforting effects of the light sleet that began falling a half-hour earlier and could no longer be ignored.

The wagon drivers had taken it on themselves to brew up some hot morning java, the women having had the sense to bring appropriate supplies. As the fire sputtered into life, only a few grunts could be heard as the men tucked away their gear and took up positions on its perimeter. A series of audible sips, an uttered expletive following a spilled cup, then more silence.

"Well, TJ, look what you done got us into", drawled Shorty Bartlett, so dubbed in honor of his lanky 6'5" frame. "A week ago and I'd never yanked a trigger on nothing more than a bunch of quail...."

"Be thankful you're gonna be provided targets big enough to *hit*" came an interruption from across the fire, drawing a burst of laughter at the expense of Shorty, known to be the finest marksman in Freeborn County.

Then more silence.

December 1, 1861

The thermometer read 12 degrees next to the parade ground commisary at Ft. Snelling. A light snow was falling on the hard ground, not flakes, not hail exactly, but tiny balls of ice that rode the brisk wind that buffeted the bluff, and made a kind of rat-a-tat noise as they hit the stocks of the troop's weapons and the bills of their caps. It was 7:00 AM, just barely light, with night surrendering to the somber gray of yet another overcast and frigid day at the fort. Staff Sgt. Emelio Brooks had yet to arrive to drill his company of recruits, an exercise welcomed by the boys to get the blood flowing again after a too-long night in the barely-heated barracks. There was much stomping, and blowing of frozen breath, and not totally good-natured muttering.

This morning was different. The company had "graduated" last night from their 6-week training program, and most were now greater in their own minds. They were trained Union soldiers now, ready to take on whatever their officers required of them, though - like armies everywhere - they were not precisely certain what that might be. But they knew what they knew. Each had become familiar with his particular duties, and the tools - including weapons - necessary to carry them out. From endless hours of drilling they had become skilled at the command-based maneuvers that convert separate individuals into a single unit able to respond to the battlefield direction of one who hopefully had greater knowledge of the field than they did. They had learned to *move* when ordered, not spend a lot of time thinking about it.

The unit thought alike, and *looked* alike. Each had acquired sack-and-frock coats, the shell jacket, the greatcoat to stave off the Minnesota chill. From their outerwear to their steel-heeled brogans, kepi hats, cartridge boxes, tin plates, coffee boilers, canteens and wool knit sox, they were now all identical-appearing privates of Company F of the 4th Minnesota Volunteers, and proud of it. Self-contained with uniform carpet bag and all the supplies necessary for daily sustenance in the field, they resembled a herd of human camels, loaded for a trek through the wintry desert. Inside, their vision of themselves was far more formidable, Sheehan's more focused.

As the informal head of his small band of recruits, he had served as a private for less than a month. His corporal's stripes had been handed to him without ceremony one evening as he headed toward his barracks. His drill instructor had called his name, caught up, and handed them over to him with a simple "Here. You earned these. A seamstress will sew them on in the morning. Good night".

Not knowing if the offhanded presentation was a joke, Sheehan sought to catch the sergeant's facial expression, but failed as he turned away in the fading light. The hell, Sheehan thought. The army doesn't play jokes. Moments later any lingering doubts vanished among the expressions of support and exuberant approval of the men he had brought with him to this barren classroom. In less than a month, a primary reason for his promotion was made clear.

December 31, 1861
Head Quarters, 4th Regt Minn Vols
Fort Snelling
Adjutant Gen. Sanborn
Dear Sir:
The bearer hereof Corporal Timothy Shehan (sic) of Co. "F" is solicitous of raising a company for the 5th Regiment. He is one of our best men, and is perfectly capable of performing the duties of a commissioned officer. He has an extensive acquaintance in various parts of the state, and we have no doubt but that he could raise a company or part of one as speedily as any one. We have found him very efficient in recruiting in our company, and we believe that if he has proper encouragement he will soon be able to bring a company to the fort. We dislike to lose as good a man as he is, but we will cheerfully give him permission to go if he can thereby render better service to the government in recruiting and commanding a company than in rendering his single service in his present company.

Very Respectfully Yours
A.W. White, Capt Co
"F" 4th Regt
Wm. F. Wheeler 1st Lt Co
"F" 4th Regt

The letter produced its intended result, and Sheehan's recruiting skills were put to the test. For the next six weeks he was on his own, scouring the southern Minnesota countryside for eligible recruits willing to put their own lives on hold to halt what appeared to be the relentless advance of the graycoated hordes from the south. Through a combination of natural military bearing, passion for his cause and an Irish gift for what

Sheriff Ruble had called "tenacious persuasion", he received 22 additional commitments during the period from among the farmers and teamsters and clerks of the region, ranging in age from 17 to 36. For the last week he returned to the fort and coordinated the provisioning and early training of his newest recruits. He was going into battle, and he wanted those around him to know what they were doing.

February 15, 1862

      Sheehan's attitude toward training, his respect among his comrades and his initial success in recruiting did not go unnoticed by the command structure at Fort Snelling. With full military formality, he was called forward during assembly on this wintry morning by his bull-necked drill instructor and informed that he was being discharged from Company F, 4th Minnesota Volunteers. Jaw agape and brows pinched, he very nearly broke attention when the DI loudly proclaimed from a scroll he held before him, that: "By order of Governor Ramsey, you are ordered to accept a commission as 1st Lieutenant, Company C, 5th Regiment, Minnesota Volunteers. The transfer ceremony will be held at this place, beginning at 1600 hours tomorrow afternoon. Company dismissed!" This was all happening too fast.

      But after a night to ponder it, and the raucous and spirited support of his men, Sheehan accepted the promotion with all the gusto to be expected from a young immigrant just granted a singular honor by his adopted country. It was barely a day later when, still recovering from the excesses of celebration, the *burden* of command began to dawn on him. Just hours ago he had no responsibility but to listen, and to follow the directions of his superiors. Today, he had to formulate those directions, orchestrate the movements of some 50 men including four corporals, three sergeants, and a 2nd lieutenant, and do so without hurting - or possibly killing - those in his charge.

The young lieutenant, who'd spent the first 15 years of his life within a five-mile radius of his birthplace in County Cork, was in awe of his new country. A man with a good horse and fierce intent could cross Ireland coast-to-coast by sunset of the second day. Sheehan had wended his way westward here over a couple of *months*, and had yet to cover half the country. Apparently limitless in both territory and opportunity, America had assumed the role of surrogate God to the agnostic Irishman. He was prepared to pay it homage with every resource he could muster, including his life.

The more reports he heard of the atrocities committed by the graycoats, the greater his drive to deploy his new force against them.

But the graycoats would have to wait.

CHAPTER FOUR

On June 18, 1862, he received orders to report to Captain Marsh at Ft. Ridgely to await further orders concerning the need for his command to "protect the interests of the United States".

Fort Ridgely was a creature of Henry Sibley, Minnesota's first governor. Six years before the territory became a state, he recognized that the frontier had grown beyond the protection of Fort Snelling, and needed an outpost where the real frontier *was,* to protect both the whites from the Indians, and the Indians from the whites. His communications with both the nation's General-In-Chief and the Secretary of War persuaded them to proceed, and on March 16, 1853 the Adjutant General of the Army notified Brigadier General W.S. Clarke that he was to make "…the necessary arrangements for the establishment at the earliest practicable date of the new post in accordance with the plan approved by the war department.(.".)Construction, aided by steamboat transport, began in 1853 and continued for two years. The original plan was for a fort complete with stone buildings. That was subsequently changed. The barracks, to accommodate 400 men, was of stone, as were the quartermaster and commissary buildings. The officers' quarters were of frame construction, while the hospital, guardhouse, laundress quarters and stables were built of logs. No provision had been made for a fence or wall.

It was a nearly 200-mile jaunt between forts, on foot, with two mule-drawn wagons holding the bulk of the supplies, but Sheehan offered no complaint.. The next two days were spent organizing his 50-man troop, emptying the quartermaster's supply tent and attending to the details normally undertaken when embarking on a trip of unknown duration. With more fanfare than they really felt, Company C, 5th Minnesota Volunteers sung their cadence out of Ft. Ripley on Friday, June 20, averaged over 20 miles per day, and arrived at Ft. Ridgely late on Saturday, June 28, to be "received with many cheers".

The post commander at Ft. Ridgely was Captain John S. Marsh, a no-nonsense Union officer, age 29, who carried an aura of invincibility, and behaved accordingly. No friend of the natives in the region, he freely expressed his personal animosity toward them, more than once remarking that he hoped to have an opportunity to "chastise" them. He saw the Dakota - "Sioux" was the Chippewa word for "enemy" - as primitive, unclean and lacking in intelligence, and his own forces as militarily superior, no matter the odds. He was mocked by the Indians.

The commander was, nonetheless, a thinking leader and a stickler for detail, and spent his first night with Sheehan educating the younger man on his mission, and those he'd be dealing with to carry it out. It was Sheehan's first indication that fighting the dreaded rebels would have to wait.

"But don't let that bother you, Lieutenant.", Marsh said. "They're not going to end the war just to hornswaggle an eager beaver from the north woods; it will be there when you get through with this".

The two were sitting on the top step of the porch shading Captain Marsh's office, sipping their second pitcher of cold lemonade and keeping an eye on the swirl of activity produced helping 50 new guests get fed, watered and bedded down in an open area little more than half as large as needed. There was still grey light, the remnants of an orange sky to the west, a mist of gnats, and a symphony of crickets loud enough to fill any gaps in the racket generated by the retiring troopers. The captain slapped at a mosquito on the back of his hand, frowning at the blood that sprayed from the engorged insect.

Sheehan was tired, but the Captain managed to quickly dispel any grogginess. "You're going to the Yellow Medicine Agency. You may have to show force at the agency, because force demonstrates authority. But this action calls for a word person, not a warrior. I hope you're a good talker."

Sheehan's furrowed brow caught the Captain's attention.

"These people are called 'savages' for a reason; you don't want a lesson in why. Let me introduce you".

The captain went on for the next hour in the manner of a teacher comfortable with his topic, but struggling to keep his own biases at bay. They called themselves Dakota, "the people", he said. Their society was at least as complex as the whites'. They were all Santee Dakota. In the east, the Mdewakanton, Sisseton, Wahpeton and Wahpekute bands. To the west, the Yanktons and Yanktonais. Furthest out, the Tetons. About one in six was mixed-blood, first from intermarriage with French and British traders, then American settlers. They'd been dealing with Europeans since the seventeenth century, with few problems until their game herds began to thin out in the 1820s.

Their leaders had ridden the railroads, been to Washington, knew the power of the whites, and tried to accommodate the needs of their people with the might that was arrayed against them. But that accommodation generally took the form of yet another forced move to a smaller and less-desirable territory.

Some whites tried to help. The government sent people and money. Two agencies were developed. The

Redwood, or Lower Sioux, agency served as headquarters for the eastern reservation, primarily the Mdewakanton and Wahpekute bands, and was already well-developed with a stone warehouse, several homes, four stores, a boarding school, a mess hall, shops, sawmill and stable. Over a hundred people lived and worked there.

Another commercial center had been started up within the past year up the Minnesota River where it met the Yellow Medicine river. It was called the Upper Sioux, or Yellow Medicine Agency, and served mostly the Sisseton and Wahpeton Bands. It wasn't as fully developed, but had several newer buildings, including a hotel.

The splendor of the agencies demonstrated the abilities and resources of the whites, but it also reminded the natives of what *they* did *not* have. Some acknowledged the power and tried to join it, dressing like whites, cutting their hair, attending school, raising crops. But these "farmer" Indians were in the minority, berated by the traditional "blanket" majority who refused to adopt white ways.

Marsh paused, conscious of the concerned look of the young soldier before him, and the flood of information he'd been handing out.

"So you can tell who's friendly by the way they dress?", Sheehan said.

"That's a start", the Captain said. "But none of 'em have a *reason* to be friendly at all. The mess they're in, we put 'em in, is what most of them think. Just giving 'em a plow and a pair of pants doesn't cut it. They figure we owe 'em. And that may be true; I just work here. Either way, I wouldn't spend a lot of time turning my back, if I were you. More than one throat gets cut around here every so often, and it ain't by accident".

Neither man spoke for several minutes. The gravity of the pending mission, and its potential for disaster, began flooding over the young lieutenant. As serious as he was about his rank and its responsibilities, he knew that up until now he'd been playing "let's pretend". All the training, and drilling and advice until now had come in controlled situations. There'd been plenty of lessons about *how* to use force, but none about *when*. And always a superior officer had been within hailing distance for counsel when necessary. Now his small force was being asked to face down a huge gathering of "savages" whose primary means of survival had been delayed by the people he represented for weeks. And what he said about it there, and did there, was totally up to him. No back-up.

"Pipsqueak", he muttered.

"What?", Captain Marsh replied.

"I was just saying how I felt", Sheehan said. "First thing, I need to be clear on just what it is you want me to accomplish".

"Fair enough", Marsh said. "I'd be disappointed if you didn't." He paused. "Wait here".

The captain arose from his position on the step, picked up the empty lemonade pitcher and both mugs and retreated into his office. Within a moment a lantern flared inside, and Sheehan could see him rifling through a letter-box on his desk. Another moment and he was once again seated on the step, lantern and paper in hand.

"First thing you need to do is read this", he said, handing Sheehan a smudged sheet of watermarked stationary containing a single hand-scratched paragraph:

Special Order No. 57, June 29, 1862

1ˢᵗ Lieutenant T.J. Sheehan, Fifth Minnesota Regiment, with detachment of fifty men of Company C and one lieutenant and fifty men of Company B of said regiment, will proceed forthwith by the most expeditious route to the Sioux Agency on the Yellow Medicine River, and report to Major Thomas Galbraith, Sioux agent at that place, for the purpose of restoring order and protecting United States Property during the time of the annuity payment for the present year. Interpreter Quinn will accompany the troops.

                        John S. Marsh
                        Captain, Fifth Regiment,
                        Commanding Post

    Sheehan read the order twice in the dim glow of the lantern, then handed it back to Marsh.

    "No, you keep it", the Captain said. "You keep your orders on your person while on the mission, in case you ever need to justify your existence somewhere. Then if anybody's ass gets kicked, it would be the one who sent you".

    Sheehan folded the document into thirds, then one more time to give it stiffness, tapping it several times on the back of his left hand.

    "I notice you're giving me over 100 troops", he said. "Are we *expecting* problems?"

    "I'd use the word 'anticipate', Lieutenant", Marsh said." I pray to God that we don't, but the man is a fool who fails to anticipate. Particularly with these people."

    "Picture this", he said, leaning forward, punching into his palm for emphasis. "Indians as far as you can see. Horses and people shittin' anywhere they want. Either dust or mud at all times. Little kids crying. Every day they get told that their annuity will be here *today*; every day we look like liars. We got nothing to feed 'em. They fill up on water and a little grain. They're getting downright annoyed - and we got a couple dozen civilians up there who're looking for some protection, and let us know about *that* every day. You are that protection. Now you know everything I know."

The men spoke for just a few minutes more, the Captain terse and seemingly disinterested in providing more detail, Sheehan barely able to stay awake. After securing permission to add a third day to preparations for the 14-mile trip to the agency, given their just-completed 200-mile jaunt from Ft. Ripley, Sheehan thanked the captain for his information, and went off in search of Sgt. Kennedy and a decent night's rest.

CHAPTER FIVE

The patter of a light rain on his tarp brought the still groggy Lieutenant awake. After a quick fill of biscuits and coffee, and a conference with Sgt. Kennedy and Lt. Gere of Company B, he went off in search of interpreter Peter Quinn.

Though Sheehan was a zealot in his love of country, and courageous, he was not brash. Joining a phalanx of well armed and supplied troops in assaulting a fixed military position was one thing; pacifying thousands of hungry and angry natives with even 100 green troops was another.

During his training, Sheehan had made the acquaintance of the agency's grizzled 70-year-old interpreter, who'd visited the fort frequently escorting Sioux headmen or picking up supplies in a creaky, tilted buckboard nearly as old as he was. Sporting mutton-chop whiskers that had seldom seen a comb and a voice seemingly funneled through wet gravel, he looked the true, untamable frontiersman to the admiring 26-year-old, and something akin to a father/son dialog had begun between them.

Quinn, like Kennedy, was a native Irishman, having come over in 1835, the year of Sheehan's birth. With that common bond, a grudging respect of young Irish for their elders, and a fair twinkle in each man's eye, the pair had shared an ale or two, the occasional arm-wrestling bout - now tied at three apiece - and conversations on a variety of subjects that for some reason had never touched on the Indian population now seething just up the river.

For Sheehan, the omission was unintentional. He had clerked in a village which saw few red men, and those usually seeking handouts. His more recent focus had been on the marauders in the south. Indians just hadn't been his concern.

Quinn, married to a Sioux squaw, felt the matter best just left alone unless brought up by another. Though intermarriage was becoming increasingly common, not all approved, and those who didn't could work themselves into a lather over the issue. If insults, and the inevitable physical match-up that generally followed, were to alight on him, so be it. He would handle it. But age had mellowed a scrappy disposition. Why start what, at best, promised to require substantial exertion to finish?

The interpreter, wagon loaded, was plopping the last sack of flour on the passenger seat when Sheehan approached. It was early on a Saturday morning; cool, almost see your breath. Quinn had on his lambswool vest and a floppy leather hat with a rawhide hatband sporting what Sheehan had thought was a worn-out eagle feather, but turned out to be pigeon.

"Hello, young'un.", the interpreter said, grabbing Sheehan's hand in a leathery paw. "Hears you gonna tame the whole Sioux nation with that band of squirrel-shooters you got. Is that right?"

Sheehan laughed, relieved that he didn't have to bring up the subject, and that his sometimes-moody friend wasn't.

"Hardly", he said. "But if you've got a minute I'd sure like to get your opinion on a few things".

"When?", Quinn said.

"I don't know. We've got to move out in three days, and got a few things to do to get that done. How about now?"

Quinn paused, looked around, and nodded. "Follow me.", he said, and trundled off toward the small, converted four-horse stable that had been allotted him due to his age, officially, and the fact that he was the post's resident bootlegger, unofficially. His "office", he called it, and had carved his name on the upper half of the stable door by means of staking his claim to it. Since most on the post were his customers, no one disputed his claim.

A once-leather-covered swivel chair served as his personal command post, and he took it now, his ample butt stirring up a mist of dust and something that sounded like a rusty groan from the chair's long-since flattened springs.

"Sit.", he said, waving the younger man to a straw-tick mattress atop a built-in bench-bed under the shack's only window, and across from the desk.

"It's an honor, sir.", Sheehan said, suppressing a grin and looking appropriately wide-eyed.

"Don't bullshit me, whippersnapper. I'm a busy man. You wanted me, you got me. Spit it out".

"I will.", Sheehan said. "Getting right to it, I'm not ashamed to admit that I'm feeling a little worn. In the last hour I've had four men shake their heads and tell me to start praying, that we're about to land on a hornet's nest, and the hornets are all mean and mad and they all have guns. There's a lot more of them than there is of us, so we're not gonna whip 'em, and we'd *better* be able to talk to 'em. I'm not at all opposed to doing that, but about what? They're about to get tens of thousands of dollars. Why are they so itchy?"

The interpreter looked directly at the young Lieutenant for a moment.

"Well I guess I'm gonna shake my head, too.", he said. "You don't really know?"

"I know that the annuities are late, but that's about it".

"Well let me give you a two-minute summary about why them hornets are swirling around over there.", Quinn said, looking out the window and licking the cigarette he'd been rolling.

"It's 1862. Up until, let's see, fifty-some years ago, them Dakota ranged over an area about some 30,000 square miles, half way to the Canadian border, over past the St. Croix River, west to the bounds of the Minnesota Territory and down all the way to Iowa. Their only enemy was the Chippewa, and they finally agreed to stick more up north and east. Then came Thomas Jefferson, and his boy Pike; can't remember the first name. It was in 1805, somehow there came to be a treaty, and we began filtering in. And filtering in, and filtering in, and filtering in. The Sioux lived off the land, and the whites was taking it away - and killing the meat that fed these people for the last few thousand years or so.

"Then more treaties, and more land given up, and more 'annuities', and wouldn't you know it, the Indians were down to 5% of the land they'd had within the memory of their old people, and because there was hardly any game left, they were dependent on the people who'd taken their land for the supplies that kept 'em alive. No fewer Indians; just less game, less land - and so many whites you couldn't help but trip over 'em. The Indians was forced to beg, the whites looked down on beggars, and everybody's pride got all in an uproar. And that brings us basically to today."

"I see.", Sheehan said.

"No, you don't.", the interpreter shot back. "You don't begin to understand. It wasn't their ruined appetites that put 'em on the edge. It was their ruined *honor*. These people lived on honor. Still do. Gave their word and kept it. Wouldn't know *how* to cheat. And we come in here and just plain degrade 'em. Even now. We've made 'em live on credit. Give us more *control*. Now the annuities are two months late - so the traders cut off their credit! You want to see a people get mad? Starve their kids. Yeah, they're itchy. Every right. I don't know what you are going to be able to do, but my advice is to do it quietly. You ride in there flashing them fancy blue uniforms and waving the flag and you'll come back in a box. Whatever you do, do it quietly. Talk nice. Try to help. Remember the honor. We've taken it from 'em. Show some respect and I might see you again."

    The interpreter had started his oratory in a light mood, but now he stood, red-faced, the freshly-rolled cigarette a mound of loose tobacco in his clenched fist.

    "Sorry", he said. "Let it get away from me. But you see me point. Look in their eyes when you get there. We put that look there. And it might yet come back to sting us".

    "No need to apologize, Dubliner." Sheehan said as he arose, brushing the straw from his trousers. "I guess the problem with my own eyes is that I've kept them closed. Most of the Indians I've seen looked like scrawny beggars, kissin' ass for a handout. Never stopped to figure how they got that way."

    With that, the somber-faced Lieutenant stood, touched his hat brim and strode back out into the dust.

    "Hey!", Quinn croaked from his porch as he spat out a wad of loose tobacco. "By the way, don't call 'em 'Sioux'. It's a Chippewa word. Means 'enemy'."

    "So I've heard", Sheehan responded, unconsciously cradling his empty pistol holster. "How many enemies can we expect up there?".

    "'Bout 6,000", Quinn said.

CHAPTER SIX

◁———— *Monday, June 30. Started with detachment of Co. C. and detachment of Co. B 5th Reg Minnesota Volunteers to report to TJ Galbraith Indian Agent at Yellow Medicine both detachments number 107 men accompanied by myself and Lt. Gere Camped at lower agency distance 14 miles west of Ridgely.*
TJS Journal

The day of travel dawned, gray and damp, reflecting the aura of the marchers shuffling down the bluff from Ft. Ridgely toward the Yellow Medicine agency. In true military fashion, virtually every man had already heard some version of the task before them, though Sheehan had taken pains to withhold facts that could have had an unnecessarily negative effect on troop morale. The distance to the destination was known, the duration of stay was not, so four mounded mule-drawn wagons carried canvas and camp-making supplies sufficient to sustain the troop for up to six weeks. Not lost on observers was the cannon, and the unusual, double-locked, leather-strapped and freshly-oiled wooden trunk rumored to be filled to the brim with ammunition.

The procession, two-abreast with supply wagons roughly in the center, stretched for better than a quarter of a mile, military discipline starkly absent. Given parade ground experience, the young Lieutenant was as capable of barking cadence and generating precision armed gymnastics as any of his peers, but he had already achieved a reputation as a tolerable, even respected, commander, interested more in the achievement of mission than blind adherence to the military manual. This wasn't a parade; it was a quiet approach to an encampment of potential enemies outnumbering the troop by 60:1. The silence, the whispered communications and the constant visual scanning in all directions by all troopers were not based on orders, but on instinct. These were, for the most part, young men; fewer than a half-dozen had tasted armed conflict. Many now wished they had not feasted on the tidbits of rumor swirling about the day before.

The pace through the bluffs and lowlands was deliberate. The destination was less than a day's hard march away, but the decision was made to camp once on the way, and arrive in fresh condition the following midday.

Given the mission's potential for disaster, the campsite proved a remarkably light-hearted gathering. Questioned on the matter, Corporal Nathaniel Weiss, the company's only Jewish member and its self-appointed master-of-ceremonies, expressed surprise at the inquiry.

"Why not?", he offered. "We are trained Union troopers, and if Captain Marsh says we can handle any old 6,000 Sioux warriors, what's to worry about?" The Corporal then skillfully ducked the lone boot and handful of lighter debris flung his way, and responded with a face-splitting grin.

Both Sheehan and the interpreter Quinn were grateful for the lack of obvious tension among the unseasoned troops. There was to be no room for nervous response to what would likely prove an unfriendly reception by the Sioux. Following a welcomed rest and consumption of the rations allotted for the day, an assembly was called, and the men left at ease. Sheehan and the interpreter both clambered aboard one of the supply wagons and waited for the din to die down.

Quinn spoke first.

"Is there a man among you", he said, "who's not been in a fistfight?" Sideways glances. No hands.

"Of all you fighters, then, how many of you got into it over *words*?" Sideways glances. Nearly all hands shot up.

"A comment about your mama, maybe. Or your girl. Or your guts. Small enough, but it put you over the edge. Then its over. You wipe the blood off your nose, or your hands, and shake the other feller's, and its done. You go home, soak in the tub, and back to work the next morning. That it?"

There was laughter, then, the exchanging of knowing glances, and jibes at the man nearest.

"Well that's like what we're heading into. There'll be words, all right. And more. These people don't *like* us, and with good reason. We've stomped on 'em for years, and right now we're *starvin'* 'em. They don't pet their dogs, their old horses. They *eat* 'em. We're two months late with the annuities we forced them to take to give up yet more of their territory, and those annuities are the only thing that pays the traders who supply them with just enough grub to survive. The traders have cut off their credit because those annuities haven't arrived. Figure *that* out. You want to piss off a people? Starve their kids."

The lighthearted banter among the listeners had faded. Brows furrowed in the closest rows, and murmurs were heard.

"But we don't *make* the rules here; we just enforce 'em - whether we like to or not.", he emphasized. "And if you think I'm trying to get you to have some sympathy for our red brothers, I hope to *God* that you develop some sympathy for these poor bastards before we dribble into their camp, or you're liable to respond to their insults by *fighting* them, and that would likely get us all killed".

Quinn stopped then, glaring at those most visible in the fading light, and then said more softly "The Lieutenant wants to say something".

Sheehan moved slowly to the front of the wagon, the men now forming a near-perfect semi-circle around the two leaders. Normally good-natured, the young lieutenant looked drawn, humorless.

"Our mission is to protect United States property without shedding blood - ours or theirs", Sheehan said. "Expect to be tested. Cursed. Spat at. Pushed. Pissed on. Physically respond and we'll be overwhelmed in less time than it takes to open your mouth. Fire a weapon, even once, and you'll be striking a match in a cotton mill. It'll be a slaughter. Repeat, a *slaughter*. Blood and body parts - all ours. We can't take that chance, and it's a radical step we're taking to avoid it." He paused, looking at Quinn as if in confirmation of what the two had decided.

"We're going in empty. We're going to avoid even the instinctive reaction of a single trooper by *unloading* our weapons before we leave in the morning. We're going in empty."

Silence, then a voice from the second rank, "My God, man, it'll be suicide!"

"Not unless someone bungles this order", Sheehan retorted. "First of all, we're going in with massive firepower showing. *They* don't know our chambers are empty. You'll have cartridges and powder in your bags, but permission to fire will be granted only *after* you witness a deadly attack on a bluecoat. And the man among us who provokes it I will personally horsewhip - if we both live".

"Now strip your chambers, and turn in. No horns, but reveille at 6:00."

Dawn broke over Sheehan's encampment to the rustle of rucksacks being packed, weapons checked, cold biscuits consumed and troopers tromping paths to and from the surrounding woods. No fires, no formal assembly. By 8:00 AM the word was spread to pass single-file past a checkpoint on the Agency side of the camp for a quick inspection to ensure no firearm was loaded. Heads were shaking, but objections were rare. Faces were grim, and little banter was heard. This was liable to be the real thing.

Sheehan ordered a column of twos, with supply wagons trailing, and no bugling nor show of flags. We come as mediators, he said, to resolve problems, not add to them. Business-like, he said.

The column finally set off by mid-morning, Sheehan and interpreter Quinn in the lead, and 100+ armed Union troopers, curiously silent save for the rattling of their gear and weaponry, following. The column was shorter now, the men bunched up as if for the protection of their peers. The pace was purposefully slow, so as not to appear aggressive.

CHAPTER SEVEN

"'Bout four miles to go", Quinn offered. Sheehan was silent.

"What's happening in them four miles?", Quinn prodded.

The young lieutenant peered ahead. The column was in open country, above the bluffs to the left, separated from the sparse forest to the right by better than a mile of prairie scrub and grasses.

"I don't know", he said. "Nothing I can see".

The interpreter drew up, and turned in his saddle, speaking softly.

"That's what I mean. You *should* know. A Sioux warrior can hide himself in a shallow trench in less than a minute. We should know if they've done that. That's what *scouts* are for, um, *Sir*."

After taking a sudden interest in his own boots, Sheehan abruptly ordered the two corporals who were flanking the front of the column to proceed to the extent of sight, and to report back with any sign of the Indians this side of the agency. The column was given a 20-minute break to establish distance.

Challenging the men to "spiff up" and walk confidently when in sight of the camp, and reminding them of the need for restraint if confronted, the lieutenant and his interpreter moved out with little conversation, each with his own prediction of what was about to take place.

Within a half-hour, both scouts were seen returning to the column at a brisk pace, but without, Sheehan noted, having drawn their weapons.

They had, they reported, spotted a major dust cloud ascending beyond the rise visible in the distance, roughly a mile away. They were unsure whether it signaled the movement of large numbers of horses and men, or how far distant if might have been beyond the rise itself. They didn't want to "start something", they said.

Sheehan looked at the now quite apparent cloud, and turned to his interpreter.
"Mr. Quinn?"
"It's not moving.", Quinn said.
"So?", Sheehan pursued.
"If it isn't, what's causing it isn't either", Quinn responded. " Nobody's coming toward us. They may not even know we're here. That cloud's caused by 6,000 people walking around in really tight circles, wondering when in the hell they're going to get some relief. Maybe they'll think we're bringing it".

"That'll be fine to get us through the gate", Sheehan said. "I'm a little concerned about when they find out we aren't. Let's go."

It was an unnecessarily short mile in the minds of the green troops, who were largely relieved at its single interruption.

Sheehan was not. Within sight of the milling throng at the agency, the column was approached by a hastily-driven buckboard whose obviously nervous driver proved to be none other than the man to whom Sheehan was to report, Agent Henry Galbraith, as well as his wife and children and a substantial cache of food and supplies.

After the man had identified himself, Sheehan suppressed his both his curiosity and his rising anger, and reported formally to the Agent.

"Lt. Sheehan, Company C, 5th Minnesota Volunteers reporting for duty, sir. May I request my orders?" It didn't sound like a question.

"I have several meetings at the fort, Lieutenant. Your orders are to maintain a presence, and keep order. Be visible. These people respect power." Galbraith said.

"Do you know when the annuities are scheduled to arrive?" Sheehan queried, trying to remember which would be the important questions.

"No, I don't", the agent replied, without further explanation.

"Should I speak to the head man of the Dakota?", Sheehan persisted.

"If you wish. I have not. I'm not totally sure who that is. All they do is squabble among themselves like a bunch of women", Galbraith said, drawing a sideways glance from his formidable-looking wife, seated uncomfortably next to him on the wagon. "Just do what you're supposed to - protect United States property. I'll be back in several days."

With that, he cast a clumsy salute at the young officer, clucked to the skittish mare before him, looked behind him and scooted down the road at a brisk trot, kicking up his own small dust cloud.

Sheehan and the interpreter looked at one another, then at the retreating buckboard, then back at one another. The incident had noticeably tightened the lieutenant's gut. Before it, he had been on his way to *report* to someone, that someone occupying the superior position, and being the ultimate decision-maker. It immediately dawned on him that as of this moment, *he* was the ultimate decision-maker. It was he who stood between 6000 starving and angry natives and 100 fully-armed, green and nervous peacekeepers. He cast an eye toward the heavens, looked and Quinn, and laughed hard enough for the retreating agent to hear.

"That's him", said Quinn. "His wife obviously has the balls in the family. But damnit, it's a hell of a time to demonstrate that quite so clearly. He hasn't been talking to 'em now, has he? Then how in the hell does he know - do *we* know - what other than starving to death is bugging these devils? Maybe if we were to fix some little problems, we'd buy some time toward the big one."

"We'll find out soon enough", Sheehan responded, nodding toward the camp, his laughter gone.

There, less than a quarter-mile distant, advanced a growing cadre of mostly women and young children, pointing, some running back into the camp, obviously animated, a handful on horseback, many shouting unintelligible "greetings", none smiling, but neither were they armed.

"Column of twos!", Sheehan barked. "Look smart!"

The troopers responded to the urgency of that last command by quickly assuming the requested ranks, standing tall, eyes forward.

"Forward, harch!", the commander ordered, more quietly now, remembering his own dicta not to "spook 'em".

The column marched in cadence into the camp, Sheehan regulating its forward speed to avoid brushing up against any who failed to get out of the way in time. To those in the front of the column, the scene seemed a giant anthill, with a few residents on the outskirts, then the population thickening until the ground itself was barely visible. Mostly farmers and clerks from rural areas, never before had the troopers seen so many human bodies at a single glance. Those whose respect had been tentative no longer felt invincible.

Quinn directed the column to the agent's home without recordable incident, save the glares of those lining its path.

With the column standing at parade rest, Sheehan sought to flush out a leader among the Sioux by bringing attention to himself as leader of the soldiers. He issued commands, mounted the agent's porch to address the troops, and even conducted a quick, mock inspection, complete with stern warnings. No Indian approached.

After 30 minutes of this charade, however, a suttler appeared from somewhere, with a manner similar to that of the fleeing agent - a mixture of extreme gratitude and quivering nerves. His initial question: whether or not the troop had brought the gold.

After moments of exchanged inquiries in which it became obvious that the trader could provide little useful information, Sheehan asked about their assigned bivouac area, only to find there was none. With that option open, after consulting with the interpreter, he selected one of the few areas not occupied by Dakota lodges, a strategically desirable low rise in sight of the agency warehouse, and with an almost 360 degree view of the surrounding area.

Wednesday, July 2. Arrived at Yellow Medicine Upper Sioux Agency. Camped on high nole (sic) about 25 rods from government warehouse. Some white people, but 1000 times the amount of Indians.
TJS Journal

Most of the first evening at the agency was spent by the troop establishing their own pup-tented encampment, an east-west facing rectangle with supply wagons in the center, and the Lieutenant's slightly larger two-man canvas clearly marked by the United States flag and company guidons. The knoll on which the company camped was quickly surrounded by ranks of curious natives three or more deep, some standing, some mounted on equally-starving horses, some seated or lying on the ground. A few women were evident, but this audience was mostly comprised of men ranging in age from teens to the very old. While the resentment of the group was palpable, its expression was limited to glares, some spitting, and a few younger men who stepped a pace or two onto the knoll and pissed on the ground or the edge of one of the tents.

At once concerned with his troopers' safety and the need to express confidence to the onlookers, Sheehan authorized an allotment of jerky, crackers and water for "dinner", but ordered it consumed inside the tents. He personally made a show of yawning, scratching and otherwise preparing for bed before retiring. No one was to show themselves during the night so long as no one entered their "safe" space. It was to prove a test of wills for the young troopers, and all concerned were pleased that they passed.

CHAPTER EIGHT

There was to be little sleep. It was as if the Indians were operating in shifts, with jostling, chanting and drumming continuing throughout the night, punctuated by women's voices and the occasional wailing of a hungry infant. The smoke of breakfast fires mingled with the scent of some sort of meat cooking, augmented by the eye-watering aroma of a substantial herd of horses quartered less than 50 yards away, and the waste of thousands of people accustomed to squatting wherever the urge struck.

The first full day at the Agency was active in the soldiers' camp, less so in the wider agency, which appeared to be completely without anyone capable of making a decision.

Sheehan, Quinn and Sheehan's second-in-command, 19-year-old Lt. Thomas Gere, met early on the ground outside Sheehan's tent. Quinn was grilled on the similarity, if any, between Indian activity on a "normal" night at the agency and the one they'd just experienced. Quinn reminded them that there was nothing normal about having annuities that arrived two months late with 6000 people desperately looking for them, but admitted that the troopers' presence had not necessarily produced any more particularly belligerent behavior. The lieutenant expressed relief at that assessment, and was beginning to feel somewhat less tense than he had at his arrival.

The ring of humanity surrounding his camp had disappeared, allowing him to observe the "normal" goings-on around him. It seemed as if the camp was in constant motion. Even from the slight elevation of the camp's knoll, the outskirts of the Indian's encampment could not be seen. It appeared as if different groups had established themselves in their own areas, and the constant flow of humanity was the result of information exchange between them. There were seven distinct bands to the Santee Dakota, three from the lower, or Redwood, agency, and four from the upper, or Yellow Medicine. Add in a sprinkling of one-time enemy the Chippewa, and some Oglala Dakota from farther west, and the separation between the "farmer" and the more traditional "blanket" Indians, and it was not unexpected that no one spoke for the whole nation.

    Those who did stop did so at the Lieutenant's tent, so it was apparent that his role as leader had been understood. They would seek out the interpreter, who had lived among them and taken a Dakota wife, and ask to be introduced to the "commander". What followed invariably took on the character of a "feeling out". No demands, or even requests. Just inquiries about the unit, Sheehan himself, comments about the dust, or the heat or, at most, the sorry condition of the bony horses ambling by. Testing. By the end of that first day a half-dozen mostly older men had stopped by to conduct what appeared to be "interviews." All the men were similar in appearance, headbands, open shirts, non-descript trousers, moccasins or bare feet. While no humor was exchanged, all appeared to be respectful, if straight-faced. It was a curious process, about which the interpreter simply shrugged his shoulders.

    Thursday, July 3. Camp quiet boys resting and smoking a few inds come to visit camp requested interpreter Quinn to introduce to Comdg Officer shook hands and ho ho'd with them.
                                            TJS Journal

The Fourth of July holiday dawned bright and muggy at the agency. Quinn located two of the elders who had visited the day before, and explained that in his culture this day was the anniversary of the country's founding, celebrated with fireworks. Since they had no fireworks, the troop planned to celebrate by firing the company's howitzer. Do not worry, he said; we mean no harm, and the shells will land far away. In fact, the purpose of the event was two-fold - to provide amusement for the men, and to educate tribal members as to the massive firepower available to the troopers.

Friday, July 4. Used up one keg powder Sergt McGrue and Bishop practiced on howitzer understood it well had quite a celebration in an Indian country.
TJS Journal

The days wore on.

Sunday, July 6. Went to hear preaching preacher did well prayed for the soldiers requested God to bless them and spare their lives.
TJS Journal

As the Sioux became more familiar with individuals within the soldier's camp, their requests for food became more frequent, and more insistent.

Monday, July 7. A number of Indians and squaws come and danced close to camp and called it the begging dance looked like hell sued for murder did not like them saw the Indian who shot Mr Nobles Fat as a hog feet cut off wanted something to eat did not give it to him wanted recommendations from Comdg Officer was with Inkpaduta's band committing depredations at Spirit Lake

TJS Journal

  The days were long, hot and damp. Blue uniforms quickly turned a mottled shade of murky brown/gray when the dust floating in the air combined with the standard day's supply of sweat. Night time brought little relief. While Sheehan felt that the prospect of a trooper nervously discharging his weapon had most likely passed, he was concerned about the effects of continuing physical discomfort coupled with the sense of isolation and the strong indications of animosity among their "hosts".

  To counter these affects and fill the time otherwise available to think about them, Sheehan began holding brief formations three times daily. As the days wore on, he devised a system where each trooper, in groups of ten, would have an opportunity to cool off in the river, and cleanse the "mud" from their uniforms to the greatest extent possible. The ten would then dress in their spare uniforms, and cover the next ten who'd remained fully clothed and armed during the first group's "bath". In this way, each member of the company could look forward to cleaning the muck off himself at least once per week. The experience appeared to sustain individual morale for several days afterward.

  After the first couple of weeks, unusual relationships occasionally arose.

  Sunday, July 13. All quiet in camp lots inds prowling around about 2000 bucks squaws and papooses. Danced in front of the traders' stores called it the great buffalo dance squaws had on buffalo robes all painted on young squaw wore around her the stars

*and stripes   wanted to marry white man   Mark Greer
took her to teopie (sic) stay'd all day*
                                              TJS Journal

    By the end of the third week, the troopers had begun to share their own meager rations with the particularly pitiful who approached them, largely elderly women. With these offerings being well-received, Sheehan elected to conduct small "get acquainted" patrols in the near vicinity of camp. The forays were squad-strength, and never out of voice range with the base or other patrolling squads. In no instance were more than half the men out of camp at the same time. These were seen as particularly bold in that they were conducted unarmed save for camp knives, and the few miserable pieces of bread and/or candies to be distributed as fairly as possible.

    At first the patrols brought the braves up from whatever they were doing to stand defiantly in front of their lodges, and, in a number of cases, point their own weapons. In time, those physical moves were replaced by glares, with the forays being essentially ignored as the weeks drew on. Gradually, the underlying fear of death at the hands of enraged savages lessened, and a modestly lighter attitude settled over the camp. Later, it was learned that the fact that the troopers had walked unarmed among them had been discussed in their councils, and, along with the distribution of foodstuffs, approved.

    Over time, the camp was made more livable with proper latrines dug in the nearby trees, wash stands set up, a small canvas ramada and a more orderly arrangement of tents that had been haphazardly erected in the dark that first night.

Occasionally, riders and wagons would arrive from Ft.Ridgely with the usual excitement, and the exchange of both gossip and mail. No, the annuities had not arrived; there was a war to be financed and fought, and the delay was to be expected. No, there was no food available for the Indians. Food for the troopers was unloaded at night, to avoid a show of plenty in the midst of starving observers. Even so, the disparity did not sit well with the Indians, whose level of agitation appeared to be growing as the days passed.

Friday, July 18. James Gorman visited camp said the Inds told him they were starving said he was afraid they would cause trouble if they did not get something to eat told him could not help it had spoke to Agt he said he would give them provisions as soon as he could get them up from the lower agency.
TJS Journal

The agent had returned, but offered little to solve the problems. Sheehan had come to suspect that he was in league with the traders, whose goal appeared to be to manipulate credit in order to abscond with *all* the annuities due individual Indians.

Saturday, July 19. Inds prowling around camp begging of the soldiers for some thing to eat got nothing appeared dissatisfied   *TJS Journal*

CHAPTER NINE

At around 6:00 PM on July 20, a handful of warriors accompanied by an older man approached Sheehan as he sat at the table he'd set up outside his tent, They were ominous in appearance, several with firearms, other with knives or hatchets, all with flat expressions and hard, dark eyes. None of the weapons were brandished in a threatening manner, but all were visible. The older man bore no weapons, but carried himself with a dignity that proclaimed he didn't *need* them. He stood nearly six feet tall, with skin the color of oiled mahogany. He had the broad face, high cheekbones, narrowed eyes and prominent jaw and nose that was often featured on the covers of dime novels from back east. While his expression of the moment was of a disgruntled man trying to look pleasant, his face broadcast the ability to stop an opponent with a severe look. He appeared to be roughly the age of Sheehan's father, had he lived. While the others were bare from the waste up, and disheveled in appearance, this man was fully clothed, including the boots and trousers of the whites, a denim shirt, and an extremely soiled Indian blanket wrapped around his torso in spite of the near 80 degree temperature of a late July evening.

He extended his hand in the white man's fashion. The lieutenant noticed that his hands were both curled up in a claw-like position, but took the hand in his and shook it once.

The headman called the lieutenant by name, and said "I am Taoyateduta. There are bad people in both of our camps. My good people have been suffering with the bad for many weeks. They grow impatient. I know the power you wield. They do not, and in their impatience and their anger may act foolishly. I need your help to prevent this."

The brief oration was more sorrowful than angry. While its words carried an implied threat, its tone did not. Without waiting for a reply, Taoyateduta - also known as *Le petit corbeau*, or the Little Crow, a family designation held by his grandfather and father before him - removed his blanket, cast it to the ground in front of Sheehan's tent, and sat.

Not wishing to insult the Indian leader, Sheehan removed his boots, and sat as well.

Taoyateduta began without social niceties. He said that his people had been here for more than two moons, that the annuities had been available at the latest by July 1 every year in his memory, and that the promise of them had caused his tribe to forego much planting that would have provided them food today. The farmer Indians had applied their surplus of corn to the debts claimed by the traders, and that corn, as well as surplus grain, was secured in the warehouse right over *there*. Since the annuities were coming from the lieutenant's people, why could not Taoyateduta's people open the warehouse in advance to relieve their suffering, with payment made from the coming annuities?

The Dakota people, he said, were brave and strong, and had endured many periods of hunger equal to this one. But hunger combined with the knowledge that ample food was available within a few paces caused much dissatisfaction, particularly among those responsible for the welfare of both the very young and the very old. He paused for a moment, gazing downward, then raised his left arm and circled it once. From the second rank of the newly-forming crowd came a squaw appearing to be in her late 20s, but in fact probably yet a teenager. She took from her blouse a suckling infant, silent, gaunt, with thin arms and legs, and handed him to Taoyateduta.

"Look, It is *he* who suffers while the door remains locked", the head man said. "He and others like him, too weak to cry, suckling where no milk comes. It is he we check with the rising sun to see if he still breathes, him and those worn frail from 70 or 80 winters. When they no longer do we bury them just beyond the horse corral and then expand the corral so that the horses hooves disguise the graves and the coyotes and wolves do not eat them. Would you like to see?"

The lieutenant very sincerely apologized, and quickly declined.

Surely the whites did not *intend* to cause such suffering, the Little Crow said, but that thought was growing in the minds of the tribe's young men. He allowed as how he was growing older by the day, and did not wield as much influence as he had in earlier times. He had been to Washington. He had signed the treaties - but it was those very treaties that were supposed to *prevent* what was happening here. That they did not made Little Crow look like he had gambled away the land of the tribe for empty promises. He was seen as at best ineffective, at worst complicit with the whites, he said. He was not sure how much longer he could control men such as these, waving to the grim-faced band surrounding the blanket.

Could the lieutenant not entreat the agent to open the warehouse, and keep the traders away from the pay tables when the annuities did arrive, so that the braves to whom they applied might receive the funds, and have the honor of paying the traders themselves?

Taoyateduta had spoken softly, but in a resonant tone, and a voice slightly quivering with restrained rage.

Sheehan had been looking directly at the man - and the infant - as he spoke, but now looked downward, rocking slightly back and forth as he absorbed the quite reasonable requests of this apparently reasonable man. He replied that he admired the restraint of the Little Crow's people, and that he personally did not agree with the agent, but that he was not in a position to influence that man's decision. He was here as a representative of the Great Father to ensure the safety of government property and people.

    Sheehan sat up straighter. "But I have another role as well", he said. "And that is to protect the Dakota from maltreatment at the hands of the whites. Given that role, I will take your wishes directly to the agent today, and will personally deliver his response to you at this place at the same time tomorrow".

    The head man looked away, beckoned, then returned the still baby to its mother. With hands placed deliberately on knees he sat still for more than a minute, cocking his head, eyeing the young lieutenant. The look was returned. Little Crow then arose in a single motion, and nodded his head once. Gathering his blanket, he said simply "I will sit with you", then turned, and walked with his men into the now blood-red haze of the setting sun. The whole conference, hours long in Sheehan's view, had taken just over 15 minutes.

    As he sat with his aides to review the meeting, Sheehan was struck by the danger in which he had unintentionally placed himself, Lt. Gere and interpreter Quinn. These three alone had been visible to the throng of angry and fully-armed warriors surrounding the conference. Had it gone poorly, the price paid could have been substantial. His apologies to the two men were met with a twinkle in the interpreter's eye.

"Not to worry, sir. The braves looked a little fidgety, sir, and so precautions were taken". Looking toward the nearest row of pup tents, Quinn said "It's all right, now", and watched as the flaps on the closest six opened to reveal two fully-armed sharpshooters in each.

"Seemed like the thing to do", he said sheepishly.

Sheehan's dressing-down of the troops involved lacked a bit of the pepper he'd sometimes been accused of applying when discussing matters of general discipline - particularly that of disobeying an order. In fact, extra rations were issued to the group that evening - immediately following an inspection to ensure that, at that moment at least, all chambers were empty of powder and shot.

CHAPTER TEN

Early the next morning, Sheehan, Gere and Quinn paid the agent a visit.

Thomas Galbraith was a political appointee to the position of Indian Agent, and felt by most to be incompetent - if not dangerous - in that role. From the first, the Agent had had challenges to overcome, but ignored them. He replaced Agent Joseph Brown, someone the Sioux had known since he had been granted the contract to deliver mail to Fort Ridgely nine years earlier. Brown had defended the Indians' interests even before he had been appointed agent in 1858. He valued their lands fairly for treaty purposes, even though Congress arbitrarily slashed those figures after the treaty had been signed. He kept up his calls for fair treatment. He respected their customs and understood their differences. Though white, he was a known quantity, one of the few whites the Indians felt they could trust. They thought his removal was just another in what to many of them had become an endless line of insults.

Galbraith was called by one observer a man "*supremely confident of his own rectitude, scornful of advice, inclined to oversimplify situations, and doggedly determined to cling to his interpretations of a situation, and to justify his course of action afterward, regardless of the consequences*". He was an arrogant, smaller man, with a plumpish face, thinning hair and a fondness for demon rum. He was disgusted by the native population, and he had become the only white man they could appeal to for relief.

Sheehan's efforts to change that began on the stoop of the agent's fine brick house, the agent not wanting to soil the carpets inside.

While Lt. Gere stood mostly as an observer and to add "mass" to the requesting party, Sheehan and his interpreter lost no time in presenting to the agent a list of their observations, including Little Crow's admonition, the butchering of a horse, finding the skeletal remains of a young dog, infants unable to suckle from mothers gone dry from lack of nutrition, the burial of at least two elders from what could be nothing less than intentional starvation, and the increasingly hostile signals they were receiving even from Indians they'd been able to communicate with in the weeks after their arrival.

There was grain in the warehouse, thousands of bitter and mistrustful natives starving literally within sight of that warehouse, and Galbraith held the key.

Nothing seemed to move the agent, who wielded his power as a weapon. Doodling with a stick in the dust, he would nod occasionally, then move his head from side to side rhythmically, as if in cadence to the words being spoken. That soon became enough for Sheehan.

"Major, I see I'm not getting through", he said. "Let me say it so you can understand. The Indians aren't starving because of something *they* did. The missing annuities are *our* doing, not theirs. There are 6,000 of them lining up to bust open the warehouse and take what they think is theirs. There are a hundred of us to prevent that. One hundred with much to lose. Six thousand with nothing to lose. As commander of this unit, I can no longer guarantee your safety, or that of your family or the other whites at the agency if you do not provide them with at least partial provisions within the next 24 hours. Do you understand what I'm saying?"

The agent stopped moving his head, but did not look up for several moments. When he did, his face was mottled and red.

"Then you send someone who *can*!", he blurted. He rose, threw his stick, turned and stomped back into his house.

Lt. Gere looked down at the still-sitting Sheehan. He had been certain that if the agent had seen and heard what the three of them had been living with for the past weeks, he could not have refused their formal request to avoid mayhem. He shook his head and started to walk away until Sheehan called him back.

"Sit here, Lieutenant", he said. "We're going nowhere until this baboon changes his mind".

For the next 45 minutes, the trio discussed the options available to them, all complicated by the fact that while Agent was a political appointment, it came with the rank of Major, and to directly disobey a lawful order from a superior officer would place both Sheehan and Gere in jeopardy of court martial.

They were committed to meet with Taoyateduta the following day, and felt that to simply state that there was no change would be to challenge the headman's ability to rein in his younger warriors, if he didn't lead them himself. At the very least it would illustrate that Sheehan was truly without power, and therefore without the need for respect. Their one communications link would likely be severed.

"We could bust the lock ourselves tonight", Quinn offered. "We could give 'em an hour in there and then come on 'em with a great hue and cry."

"And now do you suppose the starving masses, their women and children and old folks standing by with their hands out, would just melt away when our pitiful little band came on the scene?", Sheehan responded. "Have you noticed just how many of the young bucks are sportin' their own rifles?"

After further discussion, Sheehan brought up the Army regulation that, under strict circumstances, allows a junior officer to declare a senior officer to be unfit, and lead what would be in effect a mutiny, with the junior officer assuming command. But he didn't know just what those circumstances were. He *did* know that such an effort in a time of war could place its perpetrator in front of a firing squad.

The group's discussion was becoming louder and more urgent when the door to the house flew open, and a grim-faced agent stepped out and said "Enough!". He had reconsidered, Galbraith said. He would open the warehouse for an interim serving of provisions per family, but only after he conducted a full census, and only if they would then return to tend their own crops until the annuities arrived.

And when would the census be taken? Beginning tomorrow, the agent said. The "savages" would have to line up on the open field to the west of the warehouse; each person counted would receive a paper chit authorizing them to draw rations as soon as the census was completed. They were to line up by band. No chit, no food, and no food at all until all were counted.

The agent's order to put the milling throng through yet another humiliation brought Sheehan to the brink of risking that firing squad, but he quickly calmed down enough to agree to the agent's demand if the distribution would be guaranteed to begin at the end of the second day of the census, even if all had *not* been counted. Galbraith reluctantly agreed.

"Face-saving bastard", Quinn spat out as the three returned to their camp. "One day he'll be tossed out of that office, and I'll be visitin' him that same day".

Monday, July 21. Camp quiet in good order consulted with Lieut Gere and requested him to go with me and talk with the Agt about issuing provisions to the Inds Agt said he would soon count them issue them provisions and send them back to take care of their crops and have them stay until he would send for them to receive their pay.

TJS Journal

That night, after evening formation, Sheehan went over what he was going to say to the Indian leader the following morning, and the information he had gathered on the man since receiving this assignment nearly two months earlier.

Taoyateduta was part of a Santee Dakota leadership dynasty that began with his grandfather, Cetanwakanmani, also known as the Little Crow, who signed the nation's first treaty with the whites with Zebulon Pike in 1805. It was a one-sided treaty - 200,000 acres for $2,000 and several barrels of whiskey. Seven years later he fought for the British against the Americans in the War of 1812.

Taoyateduta was born in 1810 in the village of Kaposia, located in the lush countryside just north of the confluence of the Mississippi and St. Croix rivers. He suffered no want in his early years. He was taught to accept responsibility, and to work for the welfare of the band, and the tribe. He was assigned his Dakota name, which meant His Red Nation. He was on a preordained path toward leadership, until he turned off it.

He had been in line for the village chieftanship held by his father, but proved to be irresponsible as a young man, leaving his father's side and living with relatives in Dakota Territory. He became a womanizer, and was accused of participation in the illegal whiskey trade. He was glib and confident, but undisciplined, strong and courageous, but without vision. And though lacking in direction, he was an astute politician, and developed many allies and friends during his youthful travels.

Taoyateduta's father was Big Thunder, who carried on the tradition of Cetanwakanmani as a warrior/diplomat, accepting the inevitable onslaught of the whites for the tribe while rejecting it for himself. The chief's aversion to farming proved prophetic. On a blustery day in 1845, while helping with the harvest, he pulled his shotgun from a wagon barrel-first. The trigger caught on a protruding nail, the weapon discharged, and Big Thunder fell with a gaping wound in his abdomen. Though mortally wounded, he remained conscious long enough to deal with the question of succession. He'd fathered 10 sons, most now gone. The latest two were killed on a war mission he had initiated four years earlier against the Ojibway. Next in line was Taoyateduta, but he was nowhere to be found, and had not had the benefit of his father's counsel for the past several years. Two sons, half-brothers to Taoyateduta, had remained at their father's side. Reluctantly, though he chastised his fourth son for his drinking and bad habits, he bequeathed his chief's medals to the older of the two, symbolic of the transfer of authority. Moments later, he was gone.

Within hours, Taoyateduta had heard of his father's death, and prepared to return to Kaposia to claim the office he felt rightly his. When he heard that the honor had gone to his younger half-brother, he became enraged, and vowed to wrest it from him.

Though fierce once committed, the younger Little Crow was not an impulsive man. On this occasion he waited an entire winter, until the ice had cleared from the rivers in the Spring of 1846. The second half-brother had joined the usurper, and both sent word that the prodigal warrior had lost not only his right to the chieftanship, but to return to his home village at all. This was publicly communicated by voice along the length of the Minnesota River all the way from Kaposia to Lac qui Parle. As such, it became a public challenge, one that required the strongest response.

By Spring, Taoyateduta had attracted to his cause the family and friends he'd been cultivating all the years before. When he started downriver to claim his right, he was flanked by a flotilla of canoes from Lac qui Parle and villages along the route, including those of Shakopee and Black Dog. News of his arrival preceded him along land routes, and a large and vocal gathering faced him as he pulled up to Kaposia. His half-brothers stood before the crowd, unceremoniously informing him that he was no longer wanted there, and that if he stepped ashore he would be shot.

Hesitating but for a moment, the leader-to-be stepped out of the lead canoe onto the grassy bank. Folding his arms before him, he said "Shoot, then, where all can see". One of the brothers did. A shot rang out, and Taoyateduta fell into the arms of his chief soldier. The ball had shattered both forearms and lodged in the flesh of his breast. Immediately, following an angry exchange between the followers of both sides, he was placed back in his canoe and transported at a furious pace to the post infirmary at Ft. Snelling. Noting the extent of the damage on the nerves below the wounds, the post surgeon recommended that both hands be amputated. The Indian vehemently refused.

Following the best treatment the solders could offer, he was returned to his village, treated by shamans, and closely guarded during a long healing process that left his hands permanently clawed. Though shot, his courage in facing gunfire unarmed then returning to the scene of the assault soon after won him the support of village elders.

    Shortly after that support materialized, Taoyateduta cemented a growing reputation for ruthlessness by having both of his half-brothers bound and executed. It was then that he assumed the hereditary name of Little Crow. It was thought that the name had stemmed from a family tradition of wearing crow wings or carcasses on the belt, though it could have symbolized the darkness endured by the family. During the decade of the 1840s alone Little Crow's two older brothers were killed in combat, his father killed himself, he killed two of his half-brothers, and two more brothers and two sisters committed suicide. He was no stranger to mayhem.

CHAPTER ELEVEN

The following ~~morning dawned~~ (EVENING REMAINED) hot, with the scent of rain on the air. Sheehan, Quinn and Gere had prepared for the meeting by placing four camp stools in a semi-circle outside Sheehan's tent, and placing a bowl of bread and hominy on the stool reserved for Little Crow. None of them were comfortable with the news they had for this Indian leader.

In the first of many surprises in dealing with the headman, Little Crow arrived precisely on schedule - and alone. The only change, and it became a significant one as the days progressed, was that he was now dressed fully as a traditional "blanket" Indian. He wore moccasins that stretched well up the calf, well-worn leather leggings, a breechclout, a nondescript blouse and that same blanket over his shoulder. He had arranged his black hair into a topknot, into which a single feather had been placed. Without speaking, he looked at his appointed camp stool and food, shook his head, spread his blanket, and sat.

He spoke first, chiding the three. He had come alone, he said, to avoid frightening the men in those little tents. He did not believe that "one old Indian" should cause the white troopers hearts to race, or their trigger fingers to tighten. He had come to secure food for his people, not scalps. As for the meager offering on the stool, how could he eat in sight of those who had not? He spoke as if a father correcting his errant children, evenly, softly, with just the hint of a glint in his eye. It was an expression that became more stern when he asked what the Agent had said.

Sheehan, embarrassed, felt the need to clear his throat. All three of them, he said, had gone to the Agent and presented the case for immediate provisions.

Without revealing details of the conversation that might have endangered the Agent without the presence of the troops, the lieutenant laid out Galbraith's response, leaving the guarantee of small-portion distribution by the end of the second day until the end.

The Indian said nothing, but drew a knife from a sheath under his shirt and busied himself scraping at a patch of hardened dirt on the heel of his left moccasin while the three Americans eyed one another.

When, he asked, were the annuity payments due to arrive? Sheehan didn't know; he had been told within a week. Is there no one who *does* know, Little Crow asked. No one who can be readily contacted, Sheehan replied. You see, there's a war going on and....

"And there could be *another*!", the Indian harshly warned. Just last night he had attended an angry meeting of his warrior society, and counseled them on the foolishness it would be to take by force what would be given to them in just a matter of days. He sought to receive their pledge that they would exercise patience, but did not get it. He was told that his people were tired of listening to him, a breach of respect that concerned him.

Would he help his people line up to be counted? He would. Tomorrow morning. But the next evening he would help his people line up at the warehouse, and if they were not freely given provisions, they would take them.

With that, the grim-faced leader arose and left the soldier's camp. For the first time in his young army career, Sheehan gave serious consideration to resigning his commision. As a civilian, he could return and *choke* some common sense into the misplaced Major/Agent.

The following morning, the food issue was replaced by an even more immediate crisis.

Wednesday, July 23. Chippawas (sic) killed 2 siouxs (sic) belonging to red irons band 18 miles from camp of almost whole Sioux Nation. scalped one skinned his hed (sic) from ear to ear bold for the Chippawas.

TJS Journal

Sheehan's troops had not finished their morning biscuits when two braves galloped into camp, each hauling a pack horse, announcing their arrival with gutteral cries that could be heard a quarter-mile distant. The pack horses held the flopping corpses of two young Dakota warriors who had been overtaken by a band of Ojibway. Both had been mutilated

It seemed the final frustration. Soon enough, news of the discovery flashed throughout the agency grounds, and the curses of the discoverers grew to a roar as the word spread. As the agency's white population sought safety indoors, activity grew to a frenzy as it seemed that every male and not a few women raced for their weapons. The noise level subsided somewhat as the milling Sioux returned to the camps of their own bands, to be whipped to a froth by speaker after speaker, and all night drumming and chanting before raging bonfires that consumed much of the agency's remaining wood supply.

Thursday, July 24. Siouxs about 1500 strong started after Chippawas heard they were on or about R Brown's farm went by camp in good order looked terrible and determined to get some Chippawa scalps were nearly all mounted on horses some on foot painted in the warriors style most of them dreped (sic) only in moccasins and breichcloth (sic) with guns and ammunition some with bows and arrows and looked as they would fight like hell   returned about 4 Ocl'k went bye (sic) camp   going home seemed tired and disappointed   did not find Chippawas as expected looked cross and vicious at soldiers

TJS Journal

Little Crow was nowhere to be seen, and interpreter Quinn advised sharply against any effort to make it through the natives' ranks to find him.

The incident had produced an already visible change among the Indians. Irritated but largely malleable before, the returning warriors exhibited a vastly different aura now. In posture and expression and attitude, these were men who were skirting their limits of restraint. Patience had been counseled, and adopted, and it had failed. Quick death at the hands of a marauding native enemy became starkly symbolic of the slow death being imposed on them by what most were by now seeing as their white enemy.

Quietly, the lieutenant had passed an order to his men to assume their normal routine, and to appear busy with their duties if any of the Sioux approached. He ordered weapons, including the cannon, to be loaded when it could be done so without being observed. He and Lt. Gere made the rounds of agency buildings, recommending that the occupants stay inside, and that any firearms be prepared for defense if necessary. At each encounter, he emphasized his order that no weapon was to be fired unless under deadly attack, and that such firing would itself likely *produce* instant death among the agency's white population.

The census to be held before provisions were distributed was to be initiated by Little Crow, but the leader remained unavailable.

The drums beat 'til dawn

The following morning was marked by an increased sullenness among the few Indians moving about, and an eery absence of the activity that had marked the days before the attack. In spite of the dampness and the heat, most of the Indians remained inside their lodges. Communication between the whites and the natives virtually ceased. For several days, an inexplicable malaise gripped the camp, much to the growing concern of the interpreter and the two officers.

Then, reflecting the Indians' lack of respect for Sheehan, two of the natives rode to Ft. Ripley themselves, to confront Captain Marsh with a question. Would the troops interfere, they asked, if the Indians were to withhold some payments to the traders once the annuities arrived? No, he said. The soldiers were there to maintain order, not interfere with the payment process.

On August 4, a dispatch from Captain Marsh alerted Sheehan to the Indian's visit. They had been respectful, Marsh said, not threatening. The fact that they had sought his counsel was encouraging, he felt. Sheehan agreed. Any sign of cooperation was welcome during those days.

Still no Little Crow.

Two days later, a group of young braves from the Lower Agency approached Sheehan as he was reviewing the afternoon formation. There were four of them. One, Walk Away, spoke enough English to advise the lieutenant that shortly a larger group would arrive to hold a demonstration, and shoot off their guns as a way to vent their frustration. He assured Sheehan that the guns would be fired into the air, and that their intentions were peaceful, meant as a way to head off any rash acts that agitators might have planned. The braves' manner was respectful, but they made it clear that they were here to inform the soldiers' leader, not ask him. Sheehan thanked them, then watched as they turned and trotted off to the south.

He immediately called Lt. Gere, the interpreter and the three company sergeants to the ramada he'd set up before his tent. He had already dismissed the agent from any consideration where matters of security were concerned. Both Quinn and Gere thought the action of the group could be a ruse to delay the soldiers' response to what might be an attempt to overwhelm them. Sheehan, sensitive about giving an aggressive signal to the Sioux, reluctantly accepted the possibility, and issued orders for each man to have loaded weapons by his side, but to continue with normal activities for this time of day. The couriers had made the arrival of the demonstrators seem imminent, but had not offered any detail on that timing.

Within 30 minutes of their departure, any questions about it were answered by the ground-shaking thunder of what at first seemed a full-out stampede. While Walk Away had indicated that "some men" would be taking part in the demonstration, estimates later put the number at near 200, nearly all mounted, naked save for breechcloths, and painted as if pursuing another band of Chippewa. The column roared past where Sheehan and his staff were standing, and broke off at random through the lodges and campsites closest to the soldiers' encampment, shrieking and brandishing their weapons as if to intimidate their own people. Sheehan ordered his men to port arms, with every other man standing at the perimeter of the camp, the rest forming an outfacing circle at its center.

Within moments, the warriors encircled the soldiers' camp, firing their weapons into the air after pointing them at the troopers, and leaning from their mounts to wave their guns within inches of the soldiers at the perimeter. Braves on foot weaved in between the riders, nocking arrows into their bows and drawing back as if to fire. Sheehan screamed at the several troopers who had lowered their rifles as if to fire.

"Port arms, port arms *now!*", he roared. "They're after *food*!".

Reluctantly, the young soldiers raised their rifles, but high enough to use the butts as cudgels if the braves attempted to break through the perimeter to their camp.

With that line seemingly secure, Sheehan motioned to the interpreter and headed to the highest point of the knoll to gain a better view of the raucous throng, and a better idea of their intentions.

Quinn was first to note the crowd growing in front of the warehouse. A group of at least a dozen braves was attacking the door of the stone structure with tree limbs, clubs, even small tree trunks used as battering rams. The door was of heavy double oak planking, nearly four inches thick, and appeared to be holding, but the ferocity of the assault appeared certain to splinter the barrier within minutes. Already a gaping notch had been broken through near the handle, and two of the assailants had been able to jam the trunk of a small sapling through it, and were straining to pry the door open.

The contents of the warehouse were the prize. Sheehan calculated that he and his troopers had been treated with a measure of restraint because of their potential for helping the natives achieve that prize. If the Sioux did so themselves, they would have need for neither the troops nor the other whites who had kept them from it. To allow them to break through would very possibly prove a fatal error.

Sheehan processed those thoughts and began moving virtually by instinct. It was all coming together too quickly to permit fear. He sent Quinn to find a gunner and have the cannon pointed toward the warehouse door. With no time to assemble his troops, he screamed at a knot of a dozen or so who had gathered around him to raise their rifles. "Clubs!", he shouted. "Don't cock! Follow me!"

Without checking to see if they were, he charged into the crowd in a blaze of anger and desperation. Lowering his shoulder, he collided with one of the smaller Indian ponies just as it was raising its foreleg, causing it to stumble and opening up a narrow channel through the writhing mass. He felt himself being hurled into that channel, and caught sight of the burly Sgt. Kennedy behind him, roaring "Get back, you bastards!", and using his rifle to shove the natives out of the way.

The mounted warriors had hung back from the door of the warehouse to avoid crushing those on foot with their by-now very excited horses. Most of those between the outer ring of horsemen and those wrenching the door were non-warriors, the elderly, and women, equally vicious in their anger, but less physical than the enraged braves. With a stream of troops filling in the gap created by Sheehan and Kennedy, a ring of blue surrounded the warehouse within less than a minute. The group of braves at the door stopped their efforts, but held their ground, glaring at the soldiers hemming them in.

Within the time it took Sheehan to assess the situation, it changed once again, with a thick ring of warriors surrounding the bluecoats, brandishing weapons and hurling indecipherable insults.

The braves realized that the troops couldn't fire without sure catastrophe, and used every means to provoke it. There was shoving, poking with the barrels of rifles, the aiming of drawn bows from less than an arrow's length away. Several soldiers were struck with gobs of tobacco juice. Pvt. Anson McPherson, walking backward, fell and was instantly set upon by three younger warriors with knives drawn. A rein of rifle butts both discouraged and enraged the attackers, signaling an even more precarious situation for Sheehan and his green troops.

  The young Lieutenant spun toward the melee, nearly tripping over a blacksmith's anvil, then stood on it and roared epithets at the braves before him while gesturing with his own rifle at the cannon on the knoll, now manned and pointing ominously at those nearest the warehouse door.

  "Pull back or I'll blow you all to hell in a minute!", he shouted, continuing to point toward the cannon. His display drew the attention of several of the older warriors; others noted their turned gaze and followed it, momentarily reducing the tumult enough for Sheehan to promise a massive assault by the forces of an angry Great Father in Washington if the natives should attempt to take by force what was to be given freely to them in a matter of days. Now, with his rifle leaning against his belt, through cupped hands he said that his local chief would overrule the agent, and release good quantities of the grain before three sunsets had passed.

  The clamor subsided another degree, the Indians' fury defused by the interpretation of Sheehan's remarks now spreading through their ranks, and their memories of the cannon's ear-splitting day-long fusillade of July 4. They were milling now, looking for leadership, their focus more on those at the head of their own ranks than the blue-coated barrier before them.

Sheehan still stood, one foot on the anvil, the other on the massive oaken stump supporting it. He, too, looked for leadership among the surly throng before him. The crisis had been quelled for the moment, but the faces and gestures of the warriors told him that this "peace" was a fragile one. He alone could not sustain it.

Acutely aware of his status as a target perched on his stump, he looked for a spot to dismount when he noted the crowd separating for an angry elder of the tribe, shirtless, his leathery face immobile but with dark eyes blazing.

"I am He-Who-Walks", he spat out. "You will be *here, by me!*", he ordered, motioning to the ground before him. Opting for humility over showmanship, Sheehan stepped down from his stump-stage, and eyed the speaker before him. For a full minute it was a contest of glares, each coming away knowing the tenacity of the other.

Gaze fixed, Sheehan spoke first, inquiring if the brave was a headman.

"I will have yours if you do not *listen*", the older man seethed, taller and uncomfortably close.

"You *see*? We are weak because you starve us, but though herded like sheep by the few, we are many. I tell you, in two sunsets we will *graze*, and if you stand before us you will be as scraps from our bowls. Hear me!"

The older man went on for several more minutes, and it later proved that this tongue-lashing, even more than the threat of cannon-fire, served to prevent what came close to being a massacre of American troops and the civilians they'd come to protect. Sheehan's head-bowed posture allowed those nearby to report that one of their leaders had verbally bested the leader of the white warriors, and that "victory" restored enough of a sense of dignity in the Sioux ranks to forestall the need for a more physical confrontation.

Turning and elbowing his way through the first rows of warriors, He-Who-Walks produced a gap soon filled with a stream of native protesters, leaving a half-dozen of the younger men, fully-armed, guarding the door they had almost shattered seemingly hours, in truth only minutes, before.

It took Timothy Sheehan several minutes to wrench his heart rate back to normal. He and his men had narrowly avoided becoming victims of the agent's policies; he would now discuss with the agent those policies.

To restore a sense or order, he formed his garrison in company ranks, then ordered "at ease", and went among them expressing gratitude for their restraint during the belligerence. There would, he said, be a change in policies soon which should relieve some of the tensions under which the men had been required to operate. Given the very real danger experienced by his command in this instance, he would investigate the issuance of a campaign ribbon for their courage and control under combat conditions. He would have more to say after his visit with the agent.

He placed the men under the command of Sgt Allie beck, 15-year veteran whom the men respected and instinctively followed. They were, in effect, to guard the guards, and to discourage any large-scale gatherings at the door of the warehouse.

Lt. Gere and his men had effectively played that role at the perimeter of the crowd, and Sheehan saw no reason to remove him from that position now.
Interpreter Quinn had coordinated the cannon placement and loading with Sgt. Bishop, and was already angling

toward the agent's house. Sheehan and Sgt. Kennedy went directly there, and met the interpreter on the stoop.

"We won't need a 'strategy' here", Sheehan said. "We're here not to ask the agent for a policy change, but to advise him of it".

Kennedy and Quinn looked at one another with barely-concealed grins. Each of the older and more experienced men had developed affection, even respect, for the 26-year-old officer over the past several months, but had discussed between them the need for him to be more aggressive in his dealings with those advocating policies that were harmful. Now harmful had almost proven fatal, and Sheehan had apparently seen the light.

Sgt. Kennedy reached the door first and, without knocking, opened it for the other two men. The agent had not been seen at all during the confrontation, and was not immediately visible in the house. Momentarily, Sheehan worried that the scene at the warehouse might have been a diversion, while other braves dealt with the universally loathed official. His fears proved unfounded when Agent Galbraith was found behind the door in an upstairs bedroom.

"I am here", he said simply, looking as if he feared violence from the grim-faced soldiers. And then, without further explanation, he handed Sheehan a memo handwritten on a piece of oiled paper that looked as if it had been retrieved from the floor of a stable.

Office
Sioux Indian Agency

> *August 4, 1862*
> *Sir. Will you accept my direction in this matter of the Sioux Agent of the government. If yes, I direct you through a reliable interpreter to order the said Sioux*

Indians to at once accept of the provisions which I propose to issue them as usual, and meet me in council tomorrow at 10:00 AM or take the consequences. I need not, I hope, assure you that I am ready to go with you or your men to any position of danger or risk, even taking my wife and children. I will not yield to them, and I must not. I want an answer.

Thos. L. Galbraith
Sioux Agent
P.S. Your place is to command here in military matters, & mine to obey.

The memo appeared to suggest an opening of the warehouse. The man, apparently having reconsidered since writing it, did not. Once assured by the men's behavior that they did not intend to beat him, Agent Galbraith became the harumphing "obstinate bastard", as Sheehan later called him, that he had always been. No, he would not give in. Sheehan's role was to "maintain your vigil at the warehouse until the annuities arrive". No appeal to common sense, or security - even of the agent's family - would break through his flat-footed resistance. Having demonstrated cowardice in dealing with the Sioux on at least two instances known to Sheehan, it seemed in an odd way that the agent was now trying to salvage his reputation by refusing to remove himself and everyone around him from very real and immediate danger while he had the chance.

A half-hour and more passed, during which all appeals were rejected by the agent, who seemed to grow in confidence as each was shot down. "I'm a major, Lieutenant, and don't you forget it. Those are my orders."

Finally Sheehan stood, placed his sweat-soaked kepi back on his head, and motioned the others up. "You are a major, Major, and thus subject to the Uniform Code of Military Justice. Courts martial. I will do whatever is necessary to save this agency from destruction at your hands, and to see you removed from responsibility. That is my duty, and I accept it with enthusiasm. Good day."

Outside, the three men stood, shaking their heads, silent, all gazing toward the warehouse with its contingent of troops, and a once-again growing assembly of Sioux who had misinterpreted He-Who-Walk's "victory", and felt certain that the door to the warehouse would be flung open today.

"Shit!", spat the interpreter, removing the ancient broad-brimmed felt hat with the bullet hole in the crown and hurling it to the ground. "Shit! The ornery little bastard is *determined* to get us all chopped up. How would he know how close they is. He never *talks* to 'em".

"Let me go in there by myself, Lieutenant", Sgt Kennedy said. "I think I can get him to change his mind. And if they bust me, they bust me; I ain't got that far to go. I could hoist his flopping carcass on that ol' stump of yours, and we'd probably all get a good cheer."

Sheehan wearily rubbed his chin, thankful for a moment of comic relief, and suddenly filled with a reserve of warmth for these two gruff old frontiersmen. They'd guided him since before he got booted up to officer, and he knew he owed them both.

"Apparently he's talked himself out of thinking this "little crisis" - that's what he called it - is a military matter, since he said in writing that I'm to command in such matters", Sheehan said. "What we need to do is persuade him that it is, and let the Indians know that that's what we're doing. I've got an idea".

It took just over forty-five minutes for the Lieutenant to send for Lt. Gere, share his idea, hear from his unofficial advisors, refine his idea, and walk back, alone, to what the little group had already identified as "the pit".

CHAPTER TWELVE

The lieutenant's idea would work only if the protesters bought into it. Sheehan relieved Sgt. Beck, and tasked him to locate He-Who-Walks. The search took the better part of 90 minutes, during which the familiar surliness seemed to grow among those jostling the troops circling the warehouse. With so much riding on his plan, Sheehan had begun to worry that Beck and the two-man protective detail assigned to him had been waylaid when the trio came around the north side of the knoll, the old Indian and what appeared to be a teen-aged warrior beside them.

The lieutenant resumed his respectful stance before the Sioux leader as the two of them sat on the stump that had played such a role in the standoff. Sheehan explained the rank differential between himself and the agent, and how he could make requests of him, but could not order behavior at the risk of punishment by his military chiefs. But he believed, Sheehan said, that his own chief, Captain Marsh, would side with He-Who-Walks' demands, and order the warehouse opened. The Captain was back at Fort Ridgely. If Sheehan were to write a dispatch requesting that the warehouse be opened, would He-Who-Walks assign two braves to accompany the courier back to the fort?

The elder man listened stoically while Sheehan laid out his plan. Only toward the end of his discourse did the lieutenant notice an almost imperceptible nod from the Indian. Questions followed, most without merit. The courier, like the rest of Sheehan's troops, had either walked in or ridden atop a mule-drawn wagon. Would he ride one of the mules back? Would his escorts be safe back at the fort? How long would it take for word to get back? What if it didn't?

The questions came faster than Sheehan could formulate answers, until he finally raised his hand and acknowledged that not all answers were known, but that neither of them wanted to see bloodshed, and this plan was one that could be initiated immediately, with answers probable within two days.

The old Indian sat silent for several moments, then slowly nodded. You shall have your escorts, he said, gesturing toward the young man with him. Your courier shall ride my horse - and he shall be unarmed.

Sheehan agreed freely, his only suggestion being that the courier be at the front of the trio when approaching the fort. He said that his man would be at the door of the warehouse when the sun touched the horizon, and that he would be prepared to ride all night to the fort. He would go now to write the dispatch.

The lieutenant had always been a man of few words, but the significance of the words he was about to write left him in conflict. In the hour or so available to him, he in fact wrote three dispatches, the first wordy and inclusive, the second shorter but more descriptive, and the third direct and to-the-point, but ending with this sentence: "If the warehouse is not opened within 48 hours, I anticipate massive bloodshed".

The courier - a volunteer, and formerly a German farmer - and his Sioux escort left just before sunset, the farmer uncomfortable astride a dispirited bay mare with ribs slightly less prominent than on the traditional Sioux mount, but substituting a single well-used blanket for the traditional leather saddle.

The sight of the three trotting off into the dusk proved greatly relieving for the young lieutenant. He had taken the first step in stripping the inept Galbraith of his authority, and had - for the moment, at least - taken the steam out of what he felt was justifiable rage among the Indians. He knew Captain Marsh to be on the brash side, but fair, and outspoken in his opinion about granting military authority to civilians. Coupled with concern for the safety of his troops and the blatant intransigence of the agent, Sheehan felt confident that his captain would respond favorably to their situation, and do so without delay.

His relief was short-lived.

Mounting once again the knoll on which his troops tent-village was situation, Sheehan was struck by how much the dilapidated assemblage felt like home. "God, don't let me think of *this* as home", he thought, while beginning to remove his mud-spattered boots.

"Lieutenant. Company."

The speaker was interpreter Quinn, whose one-man tent was pitched just to the north of Sheehan's, and offered a full view of the path approaching Sheehan's garrison from the west. The "company" was in the form of He-Who-Walks, three other braves unfamiliar to the lieutenant, all with painted faces and armed with bows, and Taoyateduta, Little Crow himself.

Rising and restraining himself from saluting, Sheehan welcomed the group and offered them chairs, which they refused. Without waiting for an invitation to do so, Sheehan began explaining to Little Crow how he had confronted the agent, and sent a courier to the fort to bring about a change in the agent's decision-making, and…

Little Crow raised his hand at roughly the same time Sheehan realized that of course He-Who-Walks would have already briefed the elder leader on all that had taken place within the past several hours. He felt suddenly tired. Why then was the contingent here?

In his dealings with the whites, Taoyateduta showed little of the flamboyance he exhibited among his own people. Soft-spoken and ever courteous, but witnessing daily the impact of what he saw as the whites' domineering attitudes and continuing deceit, he wasted little time on niceties. Sensing the momentum achieved by He-Who-Walks, he proclaimed "We will speak to the agent and the traders *today*. We will have news for our people *today*."

To Taoyateduta, it was a demand. To Sheehan, it was an opportunity to put the agent on stage before the audience he himself had created, to force him to realize both the anguish and the power of these people in a forum he could not dismiss. "Rank" held no meaning for a Dakota warrior.

To the surprise of the Indian party, the whites' military leader immediately agreed. Turning to aides Quinn, Kennedy and Gere, he smiled, and said simply, "Let's go".

The presence in the looming darkness of what appeared in his imagination to be an unruly mob unnerved Agent Galbraith from the beginning. He had spent the late afternoon congratulating himself on deflecting the demands of the impertinent young lieutenant and his savage partners, and had been settling down into a fine evening meal of venison, fresh carrots, cabbage and creamed potatoes when the entire force entered his house *without knocking*. Within a single minute the three ugliest ones with the painted faces had raided his table like animals and had taken every visible morsel of food, stuffing their faces and their little leather bags until called to a halt by their leader. The agent had hurled insults and threats until he grew hoarse, to no avail. Then they wanted to *talk*?

Taken aback by the opulence of the agent's meal in the midst of the surrounding starvation, and on quarter-rations themselves for the past weeks, the four soldiers had placed themelves between the Indians and the agent's table, but by then the food had been taken. Taoyateduta and He-Who-Walks spoke sternly to the three warriors, but as with naughty children, not armed robbers. They did not insist that the food tucked into the leather bags of the three be returned. The two leaders took nothing.

Sheehan requested that the agent send one of his household staff to bring the traders to the meeting, which he reluctantly did. Several minutes later, trader Andrew Myrick and the young missionary John Williamson showed up.

From the beginning, the meeting did not go well. The trader and the agent sounded as if they had reached some sort of pact to prevent the Indians from eating at all. Little Crow spoke quietly and reasonably, detailing the privations that his people had suffered, the fact that much of the grain in the warehouse was that grown by his own people, and that since the annuities would be here any day now - he had been told - there was no reason not to grant a few days credit; they would be getting their money soon. Or…was there a problem with the annuity money?

Galbraith hastened to assure Little Crow that there was no problem, that the money would arrive soon, but that he was "bound" not to distribute the grain before the traders could be paid for it on the spot. He was intransigent. Trader Myrick, whom Sheehan had seen but not spoken with in the past, proved to be even more of an obstruction. Little Crow, when refused by the agent, commented calmly that additional stores of foodstuffs were held at each of the trader's stores. If Galbraith were "bound" by agreements with the government not to disburse the grains, could not the traders themselves do so from their own stores?

There was a pause while this seemingly reasonable request was considered, with Galbraith eyeing Myrick in a silent request for the trader to extract them from this now awkward corner. Then Myrick, whether from frustration, anger or simple arrogance, made what was to prove to be a fatal error. "We will release nothing", he snarled. "As far as I'm concerned, if your people are hungry, let them eat grass".

The comment stunned everyone in the room, even Galbraith. Sheehan, seated across the room, hunched his shoulders and leaned forward, as if attempting to clarify the remark he had just heard. The interpreter, who had squatted with his back to the front wall, lowered his head and slowly shook it side-to-side. Lt. Gere, standing beside the front door, looked at Sheehan, then at the stone-faced Little Crow, muttered "Oh, Jesus", and walked out onto the porch. Of the five Indians in the room, the only acknowledgement of Myrick's remark came from the brave standing closest to Myrick, whose gesture toward his sheathed knife was stopped by a sharp glance and toss of the head by He-Who-Walks.

For seemingly minutes, no sound was heard from the two Sioux leaders. Myrick, now red-faced and defiant, returned their glares until Little Crow finally stood, said "That shall be known" and walked toward the door. Sheehan followed, wanting to apologize but realizing that the incident, on top of the conditions endured during the last weeks - years? - went beyond apologies, couldn't find the words.

Once outside, the three braves shouted something Sheehan couldn't understand, and sprinted toward the warehouse. Little Crow and He-Who-Walks, slump-shouldered, began walking slowly in that direction, as if wanting to delay exposing what had just occurred. The older man paused, turned to the lieutenant with a look more of resignation than outrage, and said "When people are starving, they take what they need."

CHAPTER THIRTEEN

By the next morning, Myrick's remark had reached every corner of the extended compound. The ground in front of the warehouse, emptied yesterday, had begun to fill once again. This time, there were no idle spectators. Every member of the gathering throng was here for a purpose - younger, male, some painted, virtually all armed with gun, bow, club or axe. Some were seated, in spite of the mud that remained from the rain of a day before, others gathered in small groups. All were outwardly calm. There were no apparent agitators, but the looks on the faces of those present were uniformly grim. By mid-morning, a couple of hundred had gathered, with more streaming in.

The interpreter had suggested that troop presence be kept to a minimum until Captain Marsh's response to the dispatch could be determined, and Sheehan readily agreed.

Discussions between the lieutenant and his aides about the likely outcome of Myrick's remarks had begun shortly after they were heard, and continued right up to mid-morning. None of the alternatives was positive. The whole camp had been on edge prior to the trader's outburst, and Sheehan felt that the numbness exhibited by its inhabitants now was a result of an undirected despair that could explode into rage at any instant. Formations were cancelled; the men were directed to take their rations in their tents. The interpreter was sent to try to locate Little Crow or He-Who-Walks to enter into talks that would at least have the appearance of something potentially positive. All the while Sheehan's own rage at the agent and trader Myrick bubbled near the surface. Why should these arrogant, money-grubbing political-appointee bastards be allowed to endanger his aides and his entire company? He found no answer, and stayed all morning within the oddly comforting confines of his "home" knoll, trying to bolster the spirits of his own increasingly gloomy troop.

CHAPTER FOURTEEN

Captain John Marsh was known to some as "Mad Marsh", not due to some mental deficiency, but to his invariably jut-jawed response to the various frontier irritants that seemed to beset him on a daily basis. He held no love for the Sioux, considering his current assignment as "nursemaid" to the nation and those seeking to rob them as beneath him. His irritation had been known to result in hasty decisions in the past.

Not to say that he wasn't a compassionate man, particularly where his own troops were concerned.

Lt. Sheehan was one of those troops, though God knows a green one. That's why Marsh harbored the faint stirrings of guilt for sending him on a fool's mission - nursemaiding the whole Santee Sioux nation so they wouldn't get too rambunctious while waiting for this year's federal handout. Why a handout at all? It'd just go to the traders in exchange for children's' trinkets, some cloth, a little grain and tools enough to let the savages bleed the earth beneath their feet. He forced himself not to dwell on the system that much; the more he did the guiltier he felt.

The guilt was what had kept him awake for most of the night that August 6, and why he was already up with boots on at 4:00 o'clock when three horsemen approached his barracks office at a worn-out canter. What the hell... He was about to dress the riders down when he noticed through the gloom that two of them wore blankets on their backs and brandished bows. The third was even now attempting an awkward salute, which the now curious officer returned with an equal lack of enthusiasm.

The salute was delivered by a wary and exhausted Corporal Bryan Habig, who nearly fell as he dismounted after 10 hours of flopping about on the jagged spine of an ill-fed and nervous bay mare, with but a single thin blanket for a saddle. Quickly explaining his unsmiling Sioux escort, the courier handed Captain Marsh Lt. Sheehan's scrawled dispatch, and waited silently for a response.

The Captain took the dispatch into his office, turned up the lantern, sat down and almost immediately began to level a string of heartfelt curses. *Damn* that mealy-mouthed agent! Starving? Mutiny? Bloodshed? This was his fault, the Captain assessed. He'd gotten the serious but inexperienced young Lieutenant into this pickle, and now he had to get him out.

CHAPTER FIFTEEN

The appearance of the participants at the hastily-arranged conference at the Yellow Medicine Agency was, as Sgt. Kennedy later described, garish. Feeling that this meeting would prove to be the most important in his brief career, Lt. Sheehan had ordered his aides to attend in their full-dress blues, or at least as full-dress as weeks of living in filthy conditions would allow. That it was being held at all was seen as miraculous by the increasingly tense young commander. Sgt. Kennedy had located He-Who-Walks, but his reception was notably cool. Why should he "walk in a circle", the Indian said, and give the pretense that issues were being successfully resolved, when the truth was the opposite, and the only purpose of the pretense was to delay the inevitable. It was the first hint to any member of Sheehan's staff of the extent to which the Sioux leaders felt they had lost control of their young warriors.

"That's just it!", Kennedy said. "The purpose of the meeting *is* to delay action by the young men. The solution will come from Captain Marsh, but if your men resort to violence a single minute before he has had time to deliver that solution, the outcome will be worse than either of us can imagine. In this, your highness, we're on the same side. We need *time.*"

He-Who-Walks allowed himself the birth of a smile at the giant sergeant's address. A mutual respect had developed between the two men from well before the current crisis, and the Indian leader knew Kennedy as an honorable man, if overly enthusiastic on occasion. The title had been used by Kennedy in the past, and He-Who-Walks was both amused by it, and knew the sergeant meant no disrespect. After a moment, the older man nodded, and agreed that the meeting be set for late that afternoon.

The ground before the warehouse was barely visible under the feet of what to Sheehan seemed at least a thousand natives, and his own 100-man force. In the center, a circle roughly 30 feet in diameter, were two large and colorful Indian blankets, on which sat Little Crow, He-Who-Walks, and Feather, a squaw who had served as house-servant to a succession of officers at Ft. Ridgely, and was fluent in English.

Sergeant Kennedy and interpreter Quinn were already seated on the second blanket, and the surrounding masses gave way as Sheehan and Lt. Gere approached.

The mood of the Indian gallery was more expectant than angry, and Sheehan hoped that the meeting - and its possible outcome - hadn't been oversold. His personal mood was dark. He had bought time this morning; now payment was due, and he had heard nothing from Captain Marsh. The three emissaries to the Captain had been mounted, and should have made the fort by dawn. True, there were few horses at the fort to bring back a force, but one would have been enough to get the Captain here. *Where was he?*

The answer came less than ten minutes into what Sheehan had come to view as a sacrificial ceremony. Little Crow had spoken first, calmly, explaining why they had gathered here, and what they might expect. He did not exaggerate. Sheehan, as on-site leader of the American military, was to speak next, and had risen to do so when the murmurs of the crowd and direction of their gaze turned his own to the east. There came Captain Marsh, at the head of a mounted and fully-armed squad from Ft. Ridgely, the American flag and company guidon flapping in the breeze. He had to have raided every farm within five miles of the fort, Sheehan thought, to come up with those horses, some of whom still bore the marks of harness braces. Everything but the bugle.

The lieutenant's rush of relief was tempered by compassion for the troops, many of whom were riding for the first time.

Marsh approached the circle from behind the two Indian leaders, who did not see the wink the stern-faced officer threw his second-in-command.

An admirer of rank, Captain Marsh's attitude toward the Sioux did not extend to their chiefs and head men. To these men he was able to speak honestly and respectfully. As senior American officer now present, he was invited to speak next, and began by summing up what he knew. Sheehan interrupted to expand on what he had written in the dispatch, and Little Crow watched the exchange intently as the Captain's expression grew harder, and he interrupted his junior officer on several occasions with phrases like "that's inhuman" and "the little bastard".

Finally, with He-Who-Walks deferring, Little Crow spoke again. He knew Captain Marsh, and had even joined him for Sunday services at the post a week earlier. He had, however, refrained from leader-to-leader talks, thinking that the Captain might have been part of the problem between the two peoples. Now, among his thousands, he would speak.

For the next quarter-hour he vented his mounting frustration to the Union commander, numbering instance after instance in which individual Dakota or the nation as a whole were the object of deceit, injustice or violence. Only for the last minute did he focus on the matter of his people being denied access to their own grain, waiting for payment delayed through no fault of their own.

As was his style, Little Crow spoke slowly and evenly, but both Marsh and Sheehan caught the tremor of suppressed rage in his voice. His clawed hands shook as he gestured to emphasize a point. The captain, noting the mounting tension reflected in the Indians now pressing closer, abruptly stood, nodded to the leaders, said "Enough!", and pointed toward Agent Galbraith's house. Motioning for Sheehan to follow him, he vanished into the parting crowd, unsnapping his holster along the way.

The resistance thrown up by the once-again timid agent was minimal. After unsuccessfully feigning surprise at the Captain's presence at the agency, he appeared only too eager to do the senior officer's bidding. While he technically outranked the captain, the agent knew that his was a political appointment, granted by a single-sentence letter, and could be withdrawn at any moment the same way. That, and the captain's use of the term "courts martial", melted any further resistance.

The next morning, after consulting with the Indian leaders to ensure order at the distribution point, 30 barrels of pork and 130 of flour were handed out with only minimal disturbance. The provisions somehow served to calm some 6,000 malnourished natives, and buy time for the receipt of annuities sufficient to buy yet more time. Time for what?, Sheehan wondered.

"It ain't gonna work, Lieutenant.", Quinn said as the two men observed the distribution from the knoll. Captain Marsh had originally suggested that the food be handed out by uniformed troopers, so that the Sioux could see that the US military was their friend. He-Who-Walks had objected strongly, reminding the Captain that it was the overlying threat of military power that confined the once-proud Sioux to less than a tenth of their former lands, and forced them to adopt a life of dependence on the leaders of that same military.

"And why won't it work, Mr. Quinn?", Sheehan replied.

"Lieutenant, if you smack your dog around, and you *keep* smackin' him around, even if you throw him a bone once in a while, eventually he's gonna bite you. *We* know these people are people, but the government treats 'em like dogs. Best keep an eye, I'd say." Sheehan grunted.

Captain Marsh remained visible during the distribution, standing with Little Crow and He-Who-Walks, meeting with leaders of the younger braves, and forcing both Galbraith and the two available traders - the rest had fled during the commotion - to assist in distributing the provisions. The Indians knew the men were being forced to comply, and their expressions as they passed reflected unconcealed hostility.

But looks were not Captain Marsh's concern. His feelings toward the sniveling agent closely matched those of the Sioux, and if the man was to be "spanked" by those he considered his subjects, so be it. On the morning following the distribution, with the camp quiet, the captain mounted up his 9-man pretend-cavalry and headed back at a leisurely pace to Fort Ridgely.

Two days later, on August 9, a band of 34 braves left the encampment to go to their traditional buffalo-hunting grounds beyond Big Stone Lake.

August 10 dawned quietly at Yellow Medicine, a hazy sun striving to dry up the muck produced by the previous day's spotty rains. The aura at the camp had so measurably changed that Sheehan was making plans to resume his "neighborhood patrols" when a messenger arrived from the fort with a dispatch from Captain Marsh. The messenger, 17-year-old Cyrus Cole, had enlisted *with* his horse, and thus became messenger-of-choice for all communications reaching beyond a mile or two. The Indians near the knoll eyed the sleek, well-fed mount approvingly, spurring the dismounted rider to keep a snug grip on his lead rein.

The smile on Pvt Cole's face confused the lieutenant. Grown increasingly cynical over the past weeks, the possibility that he might be receiving *good* news hadn't occurred to him. But the messenger's grin broadened as he handed the dispatch to the frowning officer, and broke into open laughter as Sheehan's eyes widened, and he followed the message with his finger to dispel any error in its meaning. Company B, 5th Minnesota Volunteers, was being withdrawn from duty at the Yellow Medicine Indian Agency, and was to decamp on August 11 and return to Ft. Ridgely.

Tomorrow!

For a moment, the 26-year-old officer shed his self-imposed military bearing, and rushed to the interpreter's tent across the knoll, loudly proclaiming the note's contents. Only after realizing that Quinn wasn't there did he regain something of his composure, and send an orderly to round up his aides for a meeting to be held in one hour.

19-year-old Lt. Gere whooped. Interpreter Quinn removed his mangled hat, looked heavenward, and said "Hallelujah" three times. Sgt. Kennedy, seated on a rickety camp stool, put his hands on his knees, pushed, and plopped backward into the still-soft soil. All wanted to read the document, and it was passed reverently from hand to hand before being deposited carefully in the very bottom of Sheehan's duffel.

Assignments immediately followed. Lt. Gere was to prepare the troops. Sgt. Kennedy was in charge of logistics - the wagons, tents, horses, ammunition, cannon and miscellaneous supplies. The interpreter and Lt. Sheehan were to liaison with the Dakota leaders, and cement relationships as best they could. Any remaining food was to be left with the leaders for distribution as they saw fit. No one was dispatched to speak with the agent or the traders.

Initially alarmed at all the movement in the soldiers' camp, the natives nearest the knoll soon went into a frenzy of dancing and drumming. Within a single hour, similar sounds were heard from the farthest corners of the camp, and continued well into the night.

By the following morning, the knoll had become an ant hill of activity. Sheehan was rolling up his tent by 5:00 AM, and he wasn't the first. Few of the troopers slept during the night, many penning letters to loved ones, some cleaning out their "rat holes", others listening to the sounds of drums without apprehension for the first time.

Packing and loading took the better part of the morning. Lt. Sheehan informed the men that they were to don their cleanest uniforms, form tight ranks, and *look smart* as they marched at measured cadence out of the agency's weathered confines - firearms once again unloaded.

Little was said during the first hour after their departure, mostly for fear of jinxing the order. Once again, Sheehan led the column, with Lt. Gere by his side and both interpreter Quinn and Sgt. Kennedy roaming up and down the ranks, answering questions from the younger men as best they could and encouraging - usually with a semi-friendly boot - the stragglers to keep up. Finally Quinn felt the need to express himself.

"Welcome to the army, Lieutenant", the interpreter rasped to the no-longer-green young officer. "At this point, I can say that you've earned that brass, and I for one am damned glad you did. You've a set of 'em, I'll say. The wrong kind of screw-up and we'd all be fodder for them mangy dogs back there. I'll say thank you, now."

Embarrassed, but pleased at the compliment from his unofficial mentor, Sheehan said simply "Nothing to it.", looked at Quinn, and both men broke down into peals of relieved laughter that lasted for several minutes.

As the miles wore on, Sheehan and his aides strode at the front of the column, though each could have commandeered a ride on one of the supply wagons. All four of the men walked easily. For the first time in weeks, Lt. Gere's expression was absent the furrows and lines that had characterized his appearance since the group of Sioux raiders had gone after the Ojibway scalpers. He'd realized then how fragile their position was among these surly and well-armed warriors, and had not slept well since. Sgt Kennedy and the interpreter were walking off to the side, carrying on an easy banter. Sheehan barely noticed, wrapped up in thought about what it all had meant, when the annuity money might arrive, what might happen if it wasn't soon, whether he had comported himself well, and most importantly, if his unit might now - finally - be sent to fight the real enemy in the south.

In this way the first third of the trip passed.

It was more of a stroll than a march. Just out of sight of the agency, Sheehan had halted the contingent, congratulated the men on their courage and their composure under combat conditions, and invited them to "join him" on their return to the fort, informal ranks, conversation allowed. He would, he said, arrange for a measure of whiskey for each of the men, an announcement enthusiastically greeted. There was no set time for arrival at the fort.

The temperature dipped into the low 70s as the sun went down, with a slight breeze from the northeast cooling the marchers as they ate up the miles. Soon enough, the sun was replaced with rain clouds carried on that breeze, and for two hours a misty rain served to ignite some traditional grumbling, but in all it would be remembered as a comfortable bit of mobile camaraderie.

Roughly four miles from the fort, the column was met by a welcome train of ambulance and hay wagons, and many of the men piled on, the hell with appearances. On arrival at the fort there followed a brief homecoming, with something of a band having been conjured up from an array of army and civilian players of varying skill levels, and a number of celebrants who'd come from the Lower Agency on a raft. 14 Sioux warriors were among that group, come to counsel with interpreter Quinn and assure all that there really had been no danger whatsoever. The message was given with straight faces, and received the same way.

The day following their arrival, August 13, the Rev. Stephen Riggs, who had lived among the Sioux for 30 years, wrote from his home in the agency that "*All is quiet and orderly at the place of the forthcoming payment*".

CHAPTER SIXTEEN

The following day, Sheehan and Lt. Gere met with Captain Marsh to debrief their extended adventure. They expressed their gratitude at having been relieved of that duty, Gere because of his nervousness - though he had performed admirably in spite of it - and Sheehan because of the zeal he carried to get on with the "real" fight. Did the lieutenants agree with his decision?, the captain queried. Yes and no, Sheehan was bold enough to offer. Yes, the agency was quiet, and the natives no longer seemed likely to explode with frustration and rage at any second. But to presume that years of perceived misery, humiliation, death, the inability to war with their traditional enemies and the abolishment of a way of life they'd enjoyed beyond the memory of generations of elders could be compensated by a few barrels of rancid flour and some rotting pork?

The elder lieutenant brushed at his right leg with his kepi and shook his head. He thought not, and was afraid that bellies would soon again begin to grumble, and now that the might of the Union Army available in this place had been tested and realized to be *not* invincible, and that the control of the elder leaders had been challenged without undue consequence, shortsighted braves might start something not readily stopped.

He hoped not, Lt. Sheehan said. He *prayed* not, and was anxious to begin his real mission. But it was too tight, and God knows what the agent might do next.

Captain Marsh questioned the two for nearly an hour, nodding occasionally, taking notes, voicing sympathy with most of the opinions expressed and adding his own color to those he thought weren't strong enough. He was a stern man, and smiled little during the interview, though he praised both for the conditions they endured and the ultimate, peaceful, outcome. The men would remain unassigned for the time being, he said, free to attend to personal matters as they wished. They were not allowed to leave the garrison.

> *Headquarters, Ft. Ridgely*
> *August 17, 1862*
>
> *Lt. T.J. Sheehan with detachment of Co. C 5th Minnesota Volunteers now at this post will immediately proceed to Ft. Ripley, and report to Captain Hall commanding at that place.*
>
> > *John S. Marsh*
> > *Capt 5th Minn vols*
> > *Comd Post*

The order to report to Sheehan's home garrison was delivered by post messenger at 8:00 in the morning, just as the lieutenant was preparing for another day of rest and recuperation. Though Fort Ridgely offered few amenities, simply being able to relax and not having to exercise the responsibilities of command had been undeniably refreshing. Though mildly disappointed that the Captain had not felt his order significant enough to have been delivered in person, Sheehan talked himself into having been feeling bored, and appreciated the dispatch for its call to action. He sent the messenger off to locate Lt. Gere, and issued orders to the younger officer to prepare the men for the 200-mile march beginning at 7:00 tomorrow morning.

CHAPTER SEVENTEEN

On that very same day, events were occurring nearby that would render the Lieutenant's recent activities insignificant. They began in Acton Township, a crossing in the road three miles south of Grover City. It was a Sunday, sunny and clear and fresh-smelling from the previous night's showers.

A settler by the name of Robinson Jones and his family and friends were celebrating the Sabbath in his sturdy two-story home, a combination post office, store and lodge located right on the well-traveled Pembina-Henderson Trail. Jones had been in the community since it was formed. He and his family were aware of the huge gathering of Dakota for the annuity distribution up the road, but it happened every year, there'd never been any bother, and none of them had any particular fear of the "beggars", as some called them. He had, in fact, served them in his store on many occasions in the past. He neither condemned the Indians nor vocally supported them. His philosophy was live and let live. Theirs', on this day, was not.

One band not at the annuity distribution this Sunday was that of Red Middle Voice, a trouble-maker even among the Sioux, who'd been largely put out from the main group some time ago. His band was at the Rice Creek camp on the south bank of the Minnesota River, above the mouth of the Redwood. Four of the band's young warriors had left nearly a week earlier on a hunting expedition to the Big Woods in Kandiyohi County. They had been specially selected for the journey because of their prowess at the hunt, and their earlier successes at bringing home critical sustenance for their band, none of whom was to share in the upcoming annuities. They were told they were "the last hope".

The four were Brown Wing, Breaking Up, Killing Ghost, and Runs Against Something When Crawling. All were in their twenties. Though lifelong friends, they illustrated the split that was occurring among tribal members throughout the region; two were traditionals, dressed in Indian clothing, and two were dressed as whites. They were still a hard trek of some 40 miles from their village, empty-handed and downcast, when they passed the home of Robinson Jones. Mr. Jones was tending the counter in his store, with his two adopted children, Clara Wilson, 15, and her 18-month-old half-brother. Jones' wife was a half-mile down the road visiting Howard Baker, her son by her first marriage, and his wife and two children. The Bakers were entertaining friends from Wisconsin, a newly-married couple by the name of Webster. The Websters were in the area looking for land to buy, in the meanwhile staying in a covered wagon near the Baker's home.

  The four hunters had found barely enough small game to sustain themselves over the past week. All the way to the Big Woods they had seen white settlements here and there, not enough yet to block trails, but certainly enough to compete for the dwindling supply of game and wild plants. The four used to feed their village from this country. Now, thanks to the white invaders, they couldn't feed themselves. They were tired, footsore, hungry - and talking about the grim reception they would receive when they finally arrived at camp.

  Jones, after he had experienced what errant horses could do to a vegetable garden, had erected a splendid split-rail fence on the edge of his property bordering the Trail itself. Earlier this morning, two of his chickens had laid fat brown eggs within a foot of one another just inside the end-post of his fine new fence. As they passed, Runs Against Something was first to spot the eggs. Looking around, he dropped to all fours, wriggled under the bottom rail of the fence and grabbed both eggs. Backing out, he stood and displayed the eggs to his companions and proclaimed "We eat!"

Brown Wing, wearing white man's clothing and generally of a peaceful nature, quickly cautioned Runs Against Something to return them, lest they all be turned in for stealing. His caution triggered a flash of anger in Killing Ghost, known to be the most violent of the four, who whipped his bow down on Runs Against Something's wrist, knocking the eggs to the ground.

"*Return* them?", he hissed at Brown Wing. "The white man steals your land and your game and you fear to take his *egg?* You are *cowards,* and I will tell everyone that you are *cowards!"*

Killing Ghost was letting off steam, but his rage connected with the disbelief of Runs Against Something, clutching his burning wrist and still staring at the shattered eggs at his feet. Without thought he clawed at the fragments, hurled them at Killing Ghost and blurted out "*Return* them? I will *kill* them! *You* are the cowards!"

With his face still flushed the young warrior brushed past his companions and vaulted over the top rail of the fence, clutching his shotgun in the other hand. Come *on,* cowards, he ordered, and strode toward the Jones' home.

The four approached the porch just as Robinson Jones stepped out onto it, rifle in hand. It wasn't that he had heard their plotting; he had just decided to go visit the folks at the Baker's place, leaving his adopted son and daughter in the house. Feeling secure in that decision, and in his daughter's familiarity with the Jones household's other rifle, he approached the four braves now standing in a group near the edge of his property. Could he help them? No. Did they have anything to trade? No, they were just returning from the hunt, and were in need of water. They were free to dip from his rain barrel, Jones said, there by the coop. Anything else? No. With that, Robinson Jones turned, waved to his daughter, and set out west on the trail to the Baker's.

The direction almost prevented the start of a war.

Because it was opposite of the way the exhausted quartet was heading, the group - too surprised by Jones' sudden appearance to react at the scene - discussed the wisdom of following. He was already too far away; someone might hear the shot. *His* rifle was loaded. What if theirs missed? But Killing Ghost would not let it rest. Cowards, he said, quietly this time. Afraid that the white man was a ghost, and would come after them? Afraid to run against something as big as you?, he said to Runs Against Something. After a few minutes of this his carping had the desired effect; the four followed Mr. Jones to the grounds of the Baker place, a scant ten minutes down the trail.

Though modestly surprised at the appearance of the four, the group at Baker's welcomed the Indians, particularly the Websters, who had never seen a Sioux. Robinson Jones was less enthusiastic, but decided to keep his uneasiness to himself given the enthusiasm of the others. After the native "guests" were given slices of Mrs. Baker's fresh-baked wheatberry bread, the talk got around to whether the Sioux or the whites were the best shots. Killing Ghost, holding one of the group's two muzzle-loading rifles, proposed a shooting contest. Mr. Webster, a member of his state's militia, quickly agreed.

Mr. Baker disappeared momentarily into the woods behind his house and returned lugging a bale of hay, which he propped vertically astride the path leading back through the forest. From a nail on the side of the house nearest the shed he fetched an old wide-brim felt hat, one that obviously had endured at least one round of seasons on its rusty iron perch. He fixed the hat between the bale strings and returned to the group, taking up his weapon, an older flintlock that he hefted with obvious pride. Jones pointed out that at this distance his daughter could hit the hat with a rock, and led the shooter back across the clearing in front of the house until the distance to the target was a good 60 yards. Proposing that a hit in the center of the hat would earn two points and in the brim one, he suggested that the members of each group take a shot apiece, with the other group scoring, and that the winning group be declared after three rounds. It was agreed that, there being only three white shooters, the guest, Mr. Webster, would take a second shot each round. The Indians were allowed to shoot first.

    The first round shot by the Sioux didn't go quite as the hosts had anticipated. In fact, there was only a single shot through the brim - and three through the center, even with the four sharing just two rifles. Well shot, Robinson Jones told the young hunters, clearing his throat and stepping to the line. Though there was jostling and boisterous laughter from the Indian group, he concentrated as well as he could on the target, and squeezed off his first shot. It punctured the bale fully three inches to the left of the brim, kicking up a miniature cloud of dust and slightly rotating the bale. Webster, assigned to shoot 2nd and 4th, walked to the bale to straighten it, and was met on his return by even more raucous laughter from the Sioux.

    The rest of the contest evolved too quickly. Webster hit the brim the first time, the center the second.

Baker nailed the target precisely in the center, offering the whites a measure of satisfaction as they walked to the now-tattered target to more closely survey their marksmanship. Turning to return to the firing line, their weapons still unloaded, the trio ran into a string of profanities from the now grim-faced warriors. Webster, half turning, looked quizzically at Jones, and in that half-second Killing Ghost raised his rifle and sent a slug hurling directly into the man's temple and out the forehead, tearing off a fist-sized piece of skull and flesh that splattered on Robinson Jones as he clutched at his falling companion.

Even the other three warriors stood transfixed at the roar of Killing Ghost's rifle and the results of his unerring shot.

"Shoot, shoot!", Killing Ghost shrieked as he jammed his rifle butt into the ribs of Runs Into Something and frantically tried to re-load, hands shaking. Almost simultaneously, Brown Wing raised his rifle and Runs Into Something a double-barreled shotgun and both fired, one slug catching Baker in the throat as he ran to cover his wife, the other passing through the abdomen of Robinson Jones, beneath the hands that were even then clutching at the gore that prevented him from seeing his executioners. Mrs. Jones, in an act of rage and courage, charged the warriors, was clubbed to the ground and shot in the back of the head by Killing Ghost as she lay face down in the soft earth.

Mrs. Baker, who had been sitting on the framework to the root cellar clutching her baby, fell backward through the opening and was momentarily stunned. She remained in the cellar, and neither she nor the baby was badly injured. Mrs. Webster had been resting in the family's covered wagon some 50 paces into the dark wood, and started for the house when hearing the initial shots and laughter. Halfway back, through a break in the forest she could see Robinson Jones, bloodied, doubled-up and stumbling, Mrs. Jones lying in the dirt, and another body. Petrified, she stood frozen for nearly a minute, then backed up along the trail, whispering "Please God, Please God, Please God…" until she reached the wagon, then turned and fled into the darkness.

As the reverberating boom of the last shots died down, and the thick pall of smoke began to lift, three of the murderers turned to Killing Ghost, as if they were dumbfounded by their own actions and sought absolution. The Ghost's eyes were wide, flicking from side to side, he with teeth clenched, growling, turning, seeking more prey.

"No more!", he roared, "No more!", raising his rifle above his head, bringing its butt blurring down on Robinson Jones forehead again and again and again.

In the moments it took for Killing Ghost to be able to respond to them, the other three had retreated back to the trail, seeking escape from the bloody clearing. He quickly joined them and assumed the lead, saying nothing but breaking into a lope back past Jones' store. As the group passed the split-rail fence, the Ghost loudly damned the fragments of eggshell clearly visible on the trail, producing bitter laughter from the others.

Clara Wilson had just completed bathing her infant brother when she heard men's voices down by the trail. Thinking that her father might be returning, she stepped out onto the porch, and saw instead the same group of Indians her dad had encountered when he'd left not more than an hour ago. Wondering why they were still here, and fiercely protective of her younger brother, the teenager stepped back inside the door, felt for the rifle leaning up against the plate rail, and stepped back onto the porch. Leaning the gun - always fully loaded - against the porch railing, she turned toward the men and in as authoritative a voice as she could muster said "Why are you....?"

Once again it was Killing Ghost who led the mayhem, he and Runs Into Something having reloaded in the event the noise of the earlier slaughter attracted pursuers. When Clara had first appeared on the porch, the Ghost had spat in the direction of the shells, muttered "Old woman, young woman", and went to a single knee before the fence, using its top rail as a stand for the rifle's heavy, four-foot-long barrel. Motioning for Runs Into Something to do the same, the pair waited for Clara's return.

The two shots rang out as one as she faced the men. Killing Ghost's slammed into the young woman just above the navel, driving her back away from the railing. The slug from Runs Into Something's shotgun struck her just under the left breast, piercing her heart and rendering her lifeless before she fell. Young Michael slept.

The opening toll of the Great Sioux Uprising of 1862 stood at five.

Continued march of Sunday aug 17th day pleasant all felt well marched 23 miles camped at Cummings farm had pleasant time all rested well
TJS Journal

CHAPTER EIGHTEEN

The miles back to the killers' camp went by more quickly than they wished, fed by adrenalin at first, real fear toward the end. As the gravity of their act sunk in, the young men knew that this was not a mere infraction, to be punished by shunning, or confinement, or beating. If the settlers sought revenge on their band, the band would take revenge on *them*. If they were caught by the settlers, even as they returned to camp, they would be hung. They were dead men. Their oppressors would finally kill them, if their own people did not. Nothing could save them now.

Passing a farmhouse near dusk, they were able to make out a man and two daughters eating inside, a wagon hitched to a pair of draft horses tethered on the trail-side of the barn. Killing Ghost halted the group, but was met with vigorous protests when he pointed through the window. No, he said, indicating the wagon. He would not kill the people inside. But they would ride the remaining 10 miles.

He approached the massive pair from the front, speaking gently, right hand extended as if holding some forbidden treat. One, the gray, nickered softly and lowered his head. The Indian reached over to rub the offered nose, then ran his hand along the horse's withers on his way back to release the wagon's brakes. A single squeak, then silence, followed by sounds of laughter from the house, enough noise to muffle the initial creak leather harness makes when going under load. One yard, then ten, then near a quarter mile by lead. As the lights of the farmhouse faded around a twist in the narrow road, all four of the fugitives leapt gratefully aboard the heavy wagon, Killing Ghost clucking the pair into a trot, then a lumbering canter, then back to a trot gentle enough to avoid unwanted attention in this region now peopled solely by whites.

Sharing a mixture of relief and dread, the four bounced about the springless wagon in silence until their camp hove into view with the first gray flickerings of the late summer dawn. The sights and sounds of their home village - cooking fires lit, dog pack barking, kids scurrying between lodges - offered little comfort to the killers. They had left seeking food. They returned bringing trouble.

The camp was known as Rice Creek. It was relatively new, established less than two years earlier under the leadership of Red Middle Voice, considered a troublemaker even among the most traditional of the blanket Indians. He and his band had been booted out of more than one camp in the recent past, and finally opted to start out on their own. They were a vagabond group, host to the Soldiers' Lodge, militant, and not answerable to any authority. But while their lifestyle was outside the norm, their needs were not - and first among them was food. When four of their best young hunters returned from an expedition into the Big Woods driving a massive freight wagon, the assumption was that it must surely contain the fresh carcasses of deer, or elk, or even the now seldom-seen buffalo, and the camp was quickly astir with hungry families eager to claim their share.

But when the "freight" turned out to be not even a single musk-rat, but four young madmen whose actions threatened to bring the wrath of the entire American military down on their heads, a number of elders returned to their lodges to secure weapons to finish the delinquents then and there. Kill unarmed whites? White *women?* Those whose blood no longer boiled at the hint of a battle tried in vain to imagine where and how they might flee to avoid those sure to come.

Incredibly, the delinquent murderers' story appeared to be finding favor with Red Middle Voice. By nature sympathetic to the outcast, the wily leader understood immediately both that there was no recalling the incident, and that the whites' response was likely to be brutal even if the four were to assume blame and offer themselves to the noose. He could sit and wait for that to happen - with his band likely to suffer a similar vengeance - or spread the responsibility while using the incident to ignite the fumes of hatred that simmered so near the surface throughout his nation.

Just to the north even now were 6,000 outraged and starving Dakota on bended knee before their despised overlords, seeking scraps from the newcomers' table, begging for what was already theirs. Would not such a force, cheated and humiliated since beyond memory, armed and well-led, be able to drive the interlopers from historic Dakota lands once and for all? Would not its rage roll over all in its path? And even if not, to halt such an uprising, would not the whites agree to cease their deceits, and grant concessions necessary for any people to live like human beings?

Red Middle Voice focused on the five whites so easily killed without any danger to the killers. Was this a sign? He knew that most of the bluecoat soldiers had been taken away to fight the graycoat whites several weeks' march to the south, and had been replaced by farm boys. If the Sioux were to be seen and treated as enemies, then let them *be* enemies while the forces arrayed against them were weakened. *This could happen!*

For hours a raucous debate raged in Red Middle Voice's camp, the four perpetrators nearly forgotten as the potential impact of the event began to sink in. Almost without exception, the elders who had followed the outcast leader warned against further violence. Turn the four in, they said. There are wise men among the whites; they would see that the murders were the act of individuals, not a whole band, let alone the entire nation. Let the lives of the killers pay for those of the killed, but let this incident show the rage boiling over in the young people as they now lived, and the need for change to avoid such actions.

But the younger men shouted the elders down, some spitting and turning their backs in disrespect. Enough!, they shouted. They were being killed slowly; they would rather ride to Wakan Tanka before this sun set than continue as dogs to the whites. The old men tried to beat the four killers with bows and sticks, and called for them to be turned over, but the younger warriors stood before them and swore to protect them even if braves from other bands came to get them. The camp seethed, and Red Middle Voice knew that he was not the one to channel its destructive energy, nor to control even his own small warrior force.

Without the customary courtesies, the unpredictable leader suddenly arose from the council he had called what seemed days earlier, shouted for his senior men and the leader of the soldiers' lodge, and ordered that every horse that could be found was to be brought forth immediately. Within an hour Red Middle Voice had assembled a small but formidable force of 30 mounted braves, enough to command attention when approaching the village of Shakopee, eight miles downstream along the Minnesota River.

The largest among the Mdewakanton at around 400 inhabitants, the village was led by Little Six, son of the respected leader Shakopee. Though he was known as

Shakopee as well, the respect accorded the son was different from that afforded the father. Little Six was an agitator. He admired Red Middle Voice, and thought like him. He, too, was an opportunist, a vengeful thinker who condemned the farmer Indians and their attempt to assimilate the white man's ways - including his own father. Shakopee, who had died two years earlier, had been a pragmatist, skilled at negotiating the best position he could obtain for his people, and above all an advocate for peace. He had thought that by passing the chieftanship of his band to his son, the burden of responsibility would temper the younger man's rage, and his tendency toward rash behavior. This did not happen.

News of the massacre preceded Red Middle Voice, who arrived at Shakopee's village with his band to the sounds of cheers, fired rounds, and the beat of war drums. Little Six greeted his compatriot with an embrace, and an invitation to council. Though acknowledging the gravity of the matter - and its stupidity - there was excitement in Little Six's voice and in his manner. *Something* had to happen, and he had no intention of being taken over the white man's knee.

The group met for hours, a raging, high-tempered appraisal of what had happened, and what was likely to happen to them as a result. The four killers were hailed as heroes and condemned as jackals who had jeopardized the very existence of Red Middle Voice's band. Once again, the arguments ranged from turning over the four and hoping for leniency to somehow turning the event to their advantage. As the discussion proceeded, the prospects for leniency grew dimmer, and the advocates for peace found themselves increasingly outshouted. Without formal acknowledgment, the question of *if* to resist changed to *when* to resist. And how.

The band's potential for success was bolstered for fully an hour by a barrage of opinions on the weakness of the American troops available to stop them. Almost all of those at the fort were fresh replacements for the experienced soldiers who had been sent to fight in the south. They were young, and had not fear shown in their eyes when defending the traders' warehouse just days ago? They were but boys, sure to crumble before an onslaught of real warriors. And horses. The Sioux had horses. The soldiers rode around in wagons, drawn by mules! And the fort had no walls! Surely, if well-planned...

Finally Little Six arose. The mood for outbreak was building, but both he and Red Middle Voice knew they were not regarded highly enough to recruit and lead the entire Santee nation. To save the few, *all* must be involved. But who could speak, and all listen?

Earlier in the year elections had been held for speakership of the tribe, the true mantle of leadership. Usually selected from the list of village chiefs, this year three candidates had been put forth - Big Eagle, Traveling Hail, and Taoyateduta, the Little Crow. Though condemned by many for his role in signing over huge tracts of Dakota land, Little Crow was respected for his courage, his family name and his diplomatic skills. But when the final vote was counted, it was Traveling Hail who had won the honor, a crushing personal defeat for Taoyateduta. It was after that defeat that he had gone over more fully to the whites' way of living, wearing the clothes, trying to farm, and living in a two story brick home built for him - except for the basement, which he had dug with his own hands - by the whites.

But farmer Indian or not, the insurgent leaders knew well that no one other than Little Crow had the respect, the motivation, and the strength to focus simmering native outrage into a weapon of war.

CHAPTER NINETEEN

Whites who had dismissed the Dakota as "beggars" and "mongrels" would not have recognized the hundred or so freshly-painted Sioux warriors who circled Little Six's camp, brandishing bows, hatchets and the occasional shotgun. The tentative beat of a single war drum had grown to a camp-wide cadence that threatened to stir the frenzied throng beyond control, Little Six realized. Night had fallen. The time to move was now.

By the time the warriors had ridden to Little Crow's house, their number had nearly doubled. This, too, was a sign. As in times past, the Sioux were becoming as one - while the whites were fragmenting, and becoming weaker. Visitors to the fort brought back tales of defeat after defeat for the Union soldiers. Bluecoats had been sent south from the fort in a stream, replaced by more farmboys. The cadre at the fort had been replaced no fewer than five times this year alone. Rumor had it that there were no more than 50 of these squirrel-shooters in the fort even now. And was not the hated agent himself heading toward Fort Snelling at this moment with a wagonload of half-breed recruits to throw at the big guns of the graycoats? Yet another way to kill those with Indian blood.

Taoyateduta slept fitfully that night. It was hot, and damp, and the canvas cover he used to ward off mosquitos stifled the breezes as well. He stirred, and dreamt visions of the humiliating loss of his peoples' land, power and respect.

The moon was nearly overhead when a growing rumble outside his home drove him fully awake, groggy, annoyed, and ready to cudgel the young men who disrespected their elders in this manner. Stumbling to his feet, he heard drumming and war chants, and through the opening where his door would one day be sighted an angry, torch-lit, weapon-waving crowd as far as the eye could see, dressed for battle and circling *his house*. The time was 2:00 AM, Monday, August 18, 1862.

Taoyateduta stood in the empty doorway, the sheen of his body reflecting the torches being thrust within feet of his dwelling. He shouted at those nearest, demanding an explanation for this outrageous display, but got no reply save for yet more screaming and angry gestures. He recognized none of those within sight, noting only that most were young, and finally raised his hands in disgust and turned to seek sanctuary in his – the white man's – lodge.

Once inside, he turned to see the doorway darken with the shapes of several men, their identities hidden in silhouette. Was he under attack? Stumbling as he reached for the rusty pistol laying near his sleeping pad, he roared "Get out!" and faced his intruders with every intent to fire. Only then did he recognize the form and voice of Shakopee, Little Six, and several others, among them leaders of the soldiers lodge and four young men who seemed anxious to remain out of sight. In just moments, more than a dozen of these leaders crowded into the first level of Little Crow's two-story house, the aroused chief standing behind the only barrier the room offered, his scraggly straw sleeping mat.

Like a disbelieving parent listening to delinquent children whose actions had caused the death of a neighbor boy, he heard the disjointed rationale for the hunters' actions, turning them into righteous expressions of justifiable frustration, and certainly a basis for war to the death for all Santee Sioux. *What?* He heard from Shakopee, from the head of the soldiers' lodge, and from the hunters themselves. He noted that Killing Ghost alone among them was without remorse, posturing like a hero rather than one whose actions had likely imperiled an entire nation. Staring, he spat at the boy's feet.

Little Crow's mind spun as he slowly grasped the gravity of what was before him, and his anger swelled as he noted that many around him had so recently rejected his leadership in favor of that of Traveling Hail.

"Why are you *here*?", he growled. What have I to do with this? Go to the man you elected speaker. Seek *his* council!".

Red Middle Voice, in the manner of a thief seeking favor from his master, shouted from his position securely behind the men of the soldiers' lodge that Little Crow was the greatest of the chiefs, and that where he led others would follow. Little Crow asked what he wanted. Red Middle Voice said to kill all the whites and take back the land.

"You are a fool!", the chief spat, "a cockroach to be ground underfoot".

Wabasha and Big Eagle stood behind Little Crow, agreeing with the foolishness of the notion that they could muster enough fighting men to defeat the might that the three leaders had seen first-hand in travels to the cities of America. Men who produce railroad engines and steamboats and cannon that knock down buildings would not fall before the likes of Little Six or Red Middle Voice or the piddling hundreds who might be assembled with little food and a few bullets apiece. It was madness. A few moments ago the chief was dreaming of ripe ears of corn and was now being asked to endorse the release of a river of blood, in which most of the Sioux nation would surely drown. He hung his head, and shook it, in the hope that this was all a horrible nightmare from which he might awaken.

The true nightmare was yet to begin.

Shakopee passionately implored Little Crow to remember the abuses of the traders, including Andrew Myrick's spit-in-the-face admonition to "let them eat grass" if they were starving. Red Middle Voice derided the efforts of the Union Army to win in the south, and pointed out the need of the Union to recruit *halfbreeds* as proof if its exhausted state. Medicine Bottle said they would not have to fight alone, that the Yanktons, the Yanktonais, the Winnebagos, even their traditional enemies the Chippewa would join them once the uprising had begun. Big Eagle said he would lead his warriors if the decision were made to fight, but that he was certain of defeat, and was opposed to the effort.

Traveling Hail said "Count your fingers all day long, and white men with guns will come faster than you can count". Tamahay, a respected elder now nearly blind, likened a war to a porcupine traveling to the end of a high branch and then gnawing off the branch he was sitting on. "This would mean total surrender", he said, "of our beautiful land, the land of a thousand lakes and streams".

Red Middle Voice, trouble-maker and chief instigator, knew that he was losing ground, that the moderates were gaining support in what had become a council for war. Befitting his status, he was in the row farthest from Little Crow, looking over the shoulders of those more respected. But he was also in the row closest to the open door, able to monitor the mood outside. Taking the biggest gamble of his life, he pushed his way through the leaders of the soldiers' lodge, and stood before Little Crow.

It was not he, he said, who wished to avenge the wrongs, to kill the whites and recover the land. Listen to the young men, he boldly commanded, gesturing toward the door with the tip of his bow. Hear them! His eyes bulging, his rage palpable, the outlaw leader was able to focus the chiefs' attention where he directed. There came the sounds of an increasingly shrill clamor for the blood of the whites, the crowd of aroused warriors now grown to hundreds, and circling Taoyateduta's home.

For moments, no one spoke, but by turns looked out of the doorway, and the three open windows on the first level. And at each other. The leaders were deciding whether to support an uprising; the warriors were concerned only with when.

Sensing his advantage from the scene outside and the expressions it generated on the faces of those inside, Red Middle Voice upped the ante one last, dangerous step. They want to kill, he said, and if the chiefs get in the way, they may be the first victims.

There was silence for a moment, due to the audacity of the proposal, not fear. Little Crow, pointing his pistol at the head of Red Middle Voice, roared that Dakota chiefs were not subject to fear, nor the mouthings of the puny. Perhaps if Red Middle Voice were to be hung from the door frame, the crowd would grow quiet!

There was so much more than frustrated ravings operating here, Little Crow knew. His people were being constantly squeezed by throngs of insolent newcomers. Hunting grounds were being consumed by fields and fencing, and what game there was was being slaughtered to meet the insatiable appetites of their tormenters. Treaty terms were ignored, with their just payments being diverted into the pockets of conniving traders. A way of life beyond countless generations was being ruthlessly stamped out in favor of plodding behind a plow and wearing the accursed white man's clothing. The band structure was being broken up. Fighting traditional enemies like the Chippewa brought punishment from government agents, even though the government itself was losing thousands in fighting its enemy to the south. Medicine men were shunted aside by Christian missionaries. Mistreatment at the hands of settlers brought no recourse from the white authorities. The harvest was bad. Last winter was severe. His people were starving....

Red Middle Voice stepped forward once again. "If you do not lead", he said, "it is because you are a coward!".

This time, the silence shut out even the noise outdoors. All eyes locked first on the accuser, then the accused. There was no movement. Little Crow had killed many in his lifetime, all of greater substance than the weasel who stood before him, trembling. But this, he knew, was not between him and the pipsqueak. He knew what had been taken from his nation, and he knew why. He also knew what they had been given, and that all of it might be take away any moment by the whim of a mightier foe. Red Middle Voice was proposing provoking that whim. Yes, many of the complaints spoken this night were true, probably *all* of them. Yes, the focused rage of hundreds of Sioux warriors would be a formidable force. *Could* they...? These thoughts and more flashed through the mind of the suddenly-aging chief as he rose to face his accuser.

"Little Crow is not a coward, and he is not a fool. Braves, you are like little children; you know not what you are doing. You are full of the white man's devil-water. You are like dogs in the Hot Moon when they run mad and snap at their own shadows. We are only little herds of buffalo left scattered; the great herds that once covered the prairies are no more. See! The white men are like locusts; when they fly so thick the whole sky is like a snowstorm. You may kill one – two –

ten, yes as many as the leaves in the forest yonder, and their brothers will not miss them. Kill one – two- ten and ten times ten will come to kill you."

Access to Taoyateduta this night had been established by power and rank. Those with the greatest of both, or direct involvement in events, now stood inside the chief's house. The same order was true outside. The leaders of the young warriors were closest to the house, some listening through the door, some the windows. As the significance of what Little Crow was saying was becoming evident, several of the leaders outside turned and raised their hands to the rest, indicating silence. Gradually, front to back, that silence prevailed. Within seconds, Little Crow's words were audible throughout much of the still-gathering mob. As if realizing this added impact, the chief's voice rose.

"Yes, they fight among themselves away off. Do you hear the thunder of their big guns? No; it would take you two moons to run down to where they are fighting, and all the way your path would be among white soldiers as thick as tamaracks in the swamps of the Ojibways. Yes, they fight among themselves, but if you strike at them they will all turn on you and devour you and your women and little children just as the locusts in their time fall on the trees and devour all the leaves in one day. You are fools! You cannot see the face of your chief. Your eyes are full of smoke. You cannot hear his voice. Your ears are full of roaring waters. Braves, you are like little children – you are fools! You will die like rabbits when the hungry wolves hunt them in the hard moon."

His words were powerful, spoken from the heart. He feared neither death nor disapproval. He had nothing to gain. And among those who heard him, whether tempered by reason or resignation, the blood lust had begun to cool. Had the leader sat after making these pronouncements, the history of the Santee Sioux nation would have changed. He did not. The blood of generations of warriors coursed through his veins as well. He, too, had been insulted by whites again and again. He had been lied to in treaty negotiations, treated like a primitive, disrespected. Now he had been publicly insulted by a member of his own band. He had yet to answer that challenge. It took only seconds of silence for that answer to well up within him, seconds which changed forever the destiny of his people. He felt flushed, the heat rising in his face. He turned, and issued his response to the insult directly to the man who had had the audacity to speak it. His voice rising in a clench-toothed growl, he pointed toward Red Middle Voice once again with the barrel of his gun, and said *"You are fools. But Taoyateduta is not a coward. He...will...die...with you!"*

CHAPTER TWENTY

It was as if a she-wolf had been tied to a tree while a trapper methodically killed all her pups, and then got loose. Little Crow may have had the beginnings of a battle plan formulating in his mind, a method of directing the rage and energy available at that moment in a way to magnify it, but he never got the chance.

The braves outside his house paused for but seconds, looking at one another to be sure they had heard what they had heard. What had come out in the heat of the moment as a response to a charge of cowardice was received by this mob as blanket approval for the summary destruction of the white race. Beginning now.

The shrieks became a wail, the wail a siren. Released at last! Free from degradation and subservience! No more being robbed, cheated, spat upon. No more wives prostituting themselves for food after the dogs had been eaten. *This* was the Great Spirit's response to a lifetime of denial of life as it should be lived. They would receive life for themselves by *taking* it from their oppressors. And in this they had just received the blessing of the one man who could bring all the bands together. No white force of farmboys could stop them.

The celebration was a release of an almost joyous rage. Until dawn the hundreds who had been drawn here ran in circles, threw each other to the ground, brandished crude weapons fashioned from the branches of trees. Some shouted the name of Taoyateduta, others – those at the back of the crowd – wormed their way forward, hoping to get a glance of the great man who had just cast off the mantle of the whites to save the Dakota nation itself. It was at once a call for slaughter and a rally to boost the confidence of those cooler heads who still feared the seemingly limitless power of the white overlords. Red Middle Voice and his soldiers' lodge leaders streamed out from the house of Little Crow to revel in what *they* had accomplished. Only one man was conspicuously absent from the "festivities" – Little Crow himself.

Within a couple of hours the tumult had died down, replaced by a silent and sinister cunning. There was no grand plan, nor time to develop one. Those who had dreamt of killing would wait no longer to do so. But there would be no "cannon fodder" attacks, as many of the braves had heard the bluecoats describing their battles in the south. With limited numbers of fighting men, the life of each Sioux warrior was important to every other Sioux warrior. The maximum penalty must be wrought at the minimum cost. There would be no whooping and screaming to scare the wits out of the dreaded settlers, most of whom carried guns even out in their fields. Besides, the Sioux were known to every white in the agency, and had free access to any building there. All they had to do was walk in.

CHAPTER TWENTY ONE

John Humphrey, 12-year-old son of Philander P. Humphrey, the agency doctor, had spent a sleepless night on the first floor of his family's cabin, tossing in the mugginess of the mid-August evening, woken periodically by the strident sound of crickets and the ceaseless whining pinpricks of marauding mosquitos. Whether from exhaustion or intuition, he felt a premonition of danger, and could not escape through sleep. Just before dawn, he quietly dressed and busied himself with work, carrying the family pails to the spring to gather water for the week's washing. Mounting a hill on his first trip back from the spring, shortly after first light, he saw a large band of painted warriors walk onto the Lower Agency grounds. They had no horses. John dropped to the ground behind a large birch just back from the peak of the hill, and watched as much with curiosity as fear. He had lived with the Dakota since early childhood, and knew them by name, knew their language. But he had never seen them painted unless they were chasing their traditional Chippewa enemies. Why were they here? And why painted?

Moving quickly and noiselessly, the group, first thought to be about a dozen but growing larger each moment, formed into separate bands and began surrounding individual buildings.

Looking to his right, John saw the agency teamster approach from the stables, leading the team of dappled-grey draft horses, already harnessed and ready to hook up to the warehouse freight wagon. The teamster, "Bear" Torgerson, did not see the two braves approaching him until they were but steps away. One of the Indians carried a rifle, the other hefted a heavy axe. Both carried their weapons loosely, approaching the teamster in a friendly manner. Young Humphrey was too far distant to hear every word, but watched as the three conversed, voices growing louder and expressions hardening. After several moments, he heard a guttural command from the brave with the axe, who reached forward and grabbed the lead rope tethering the two greys. Even in the low early light, and from a considerable distance, John could see the quick-tempered teamster's face grow a deep red.

"The hell you will", he bellowed, snatching back at the rope while planting a foot in the belly of the brazen warrior. Known for his size and strength, Torgerson's kick sent the smaller Indian back several feet, the axe flying from his grip into the tall grass beside the road. Turning toward the other Indian, Bear advanced only a step, halting abruptly as the second warrior pointed his rifle at the belly of the big man. "Pig!", the enraged brave shouted as he jerked back on the trigger of his blunderbuss, sending a 58 caliber lead ball through a column of black smoke deep into the teamster's mid-section, a mule-kick blow at a distance of less than three feet. Falling to his knees and clutching at the gaping hole in his belly, the Bear curled into a circle of flesh as the Indian clubbed him on the temple with the iron barrel of his heavy rifle.

At the sound of the gunshot, a bloody pandemonium broke loose at the Lower Sioux Agency. Little Crow's pronouncement and the braves' subsequent preparations had lit the fuse of vengeance among tribal members. With that first shot, the fuse reached powder.

With a piercing scream the Sioux who had been knocked to the ground bounded up, recovered his axe, and with the overhead motion of a man splitting a log, drove the heavy blade into the skull of the now-prostrate teamster, leaving its top third quivering at the end of a ribbon of skin, and releasing its contents in a gory spray over the hocks of the two horses. In their terror, the huge animals bolted onto and over the fallen teamster, and directly toward the sounds of slaughter that had already begun escaping the agency grounds.

The sight of the grisly scene unfolding below him brought from the terrified boy a visceral yell of fear and protest. Then, aware that he had just revealed his position to the murderers, he whirled and plunged back into the forest, sailing over the mossy tops of fallen trees for several hundred yards until a thigh-thick stub of a low-hanging branch caught him full on the forehead, and he fell, flopping, to the loamy forest floor.

He had not, in fact, alerted the killers, whose own shrieks and those coming from the agency mingled with his, and disguised both their source and direction. For the moment he was unconscious, still – and safe.

The scene he left behind rapidly exploded into a bloody bedlam. The raiders had not come to humiliate, or to otherwise chastise the whites for their decades of abuse. They had come to kill, each goading the other into more savage ways to inflict terror and agony while ending the lives of elders, infants, women – even those who had treated them with compassion and respect, or had married into the tribe. This was a rampage of the young, born into subjugation and seething since birth to get out, and of older warriors who remembered when their nation had been the most feared within hundreds of miles.

The killing of the teamster appeared to have been a signal for the general slaughter to begin. The home of the despised trader Andrew Myrick, whose "Let them eat grass" epithet had spread throughout the compound within hours, was first to fall under attack. His clerk,

James W. Lynd, stepped out of the trader's home at the sound of the first gunshot, and was nearly decapitated by a shotgun blast to the throat at close range. He was a former state senator and Indian scholar, with a Sioux wife and two mixed-blood children. He had deserted them for another Sioux woman two months earlier.

Inside, the braves detected movement, and surrounded the trader's house. In moments a rude chant began: "Eat grass! Let them eat grass! Grass!" Myrick, terrorized, slammed and locked his door in a futile last gesture of security, and raced upstairs seeking any place of concealment. He hid behind hanging clothes, tried to fit into his wife's cedar chest, and burrowed under the family bed. All were left in a frenzy of panic. Finally, the chants died down, and he chanced a glance outside the back door. Unbelievably, it was clear. Climbing over the sill, he hung down from his fingertips, then dropped to the soft soil and hunkered motionless by the house for several minutes. Finally, hearing no sounds nearby and fearing that others might hear the sobs he was no longer able to control he rose, doubled over, and began running toward a dark patch of woods some 100 yards distant.

The first arrow passed through the soft part of Andrew Myrick's upper right arm, tearing his flesh, producing a searing pain, and causing the fleeing trader to bolt upright and, inexplicably, stop. The second and third struck him, almost simultaneously, in the buttocks, generating a staccato burst of promises from the doomed man. His gaze raked the field he had just passed over, hoping to manifest rescue from any source. His utterings degenerated into a babble of sobs, prayers and pleas when it became apparent that no help was to to be had.

Warriors emerged now from the woods whose protection he sought, then from either side. Myrick could no longer speak, just holding his arms out and shaking his head from side to side. The warriors, too, were silent. Two were armed with knives, one with a scythe, the rest with bows, each notched with long hunting arrows. They started from the right and slightly behind the now stumbling victim, seeming to have silently agreed to keep the sniveling cheater alive for as long as possible. The next arrow punctured Myrick's right thigh, just below the buttock. Another struck just below the left shoulder, missing bone and protruding nearly a foot in front. The force of each nearly knocked the trader off his feet, but he seemed to think there was a chance as long as he didn't go down. He continued plodding toward the dark patch of woods.

Finally the son of one of the warriors who had directly heard the trader's "Let them eat grass" rant stood in front of the depleted figure and sent a sharpened shaft deep into the man's belly. Only then did the trader fall to the ground, rolling over, mouth agape, to receive handfuls of prairie-grass jammed down his still-gagging throat by his tormenters.

Similar acts, even more gruesome, were being perpetrated throughout the agency grounds and beyond. Traders, clerks, wives and daughters, the farm superintendent, even an elderly fur-trader married to Shakopee's mother-in-law, were all cut down without mercy by assailants they may have had in their homes the previous day.

CHAPTER TWENTY TWO

John Humphrey had regained consciousness while all this was happening, and, ashamed by what he felt was his cowardice, forced himself to retrace his steps back to the family cabin on the edge of the mayhem. Probably due to its location outside the initial ring of trees surrounding the compound – and a merciful God – neither the cabin nor the four members of his family had been harmed. All had spent a morning of terror crammed into the cabin's root cellar, and had burst forth with prayers when John's quavering voice called through the rear window. With his father in a state of shock, John sought to make up for his earlier response by assuming the role of leader, and guided his parents and older siblings silently up the hill and along the path he knew would lead them to the river. For what seemed like hours they stumbled along the overgrown trail toward the ferry landing. Gradually, the noise of the slaughter subsided, and the sounds of their passage grew louder, causing them to slow their pace while casting wary eyes into the surrounding woods.

In fact, they'd gone less than three miles when the lad's mother, in ill health, was compelled to rest in a rickety lean-to spotted to the right of the trail. The family would stay with her while John sprinted ahead to determine the distance remaining to the ferry. Within just several minutes the river came into view less than a half-mile down the path. Pausing for breath and now certain of rescue, John turned and cautiously slipped back into the thick woods. He'd gone but a few dozen yards when the chirping sound of birds came to his ears, sounds unfamiliar to the nature-loving boy. Oh, God. Were they really birds? John hunkered down, now, his heart pounding. A moment later the bird sounds ceased, and the murmur of distant voices was heard. Low, then loud, then loud and angry, then a scream, followed by staccato gunfire. Four shots, he heard, each an audible pick thrust into his ears. No-o-o, he moaned, falling to his knees, covering his ears. So *close,* so close.

Then came the trilling, the war cry, one more shot, and laughter, the brutal, gruesome laughter of primitive killers. John's mind closed. There were no external sounds, only a soft, shrill screeching in his ears. He had run, not thinking of his family. He had returned. He had run again, to find safety for his family. Without his family there was no life. Rising, without any attempt at concealment, he strode back to the lean-to. When it came into sight, he started chanting, his mind convincing him that if the Indians had heard it, they would flee in fright.

"Go *back* to hell you bastard reds, go *back* to hell right now. Go *back* to hell you bastard reds, I'll bury you, I'll bury you…". And then, his feet seeming to act of their own accord, he turned and ran.

Monday, Aug 18 Concluded to go across the country to Ripley and at 7 oclk resumed march and stopped at noon on small creek very warm and sultry after short time went on and finally camped between New Auburn and Glencoe.

TJS Journal

Of the 76 occupants of the Redwood Agency, dozens were killed in the first few savage minutes. Most of those who survived did so due to the heroics of the ferry operator at the Minnesota River, Hubert Miller, known as Old Mauley, who crossed back and forth until he had brought John and more than 40 survivors over to the Fort Ridgely side. He went for one last trip to pick up four stragglers, only to fall victim to a band of hideously-painted raiders – some said the "paint" was blood – who disemboweled him, cut off his head, hands and feet, and crammed them into the open corpse.

Those who were able to escape the initial terror fared no better. Mrs. Henderson's 3-year-old daughter was wrenched from her arms on the road to Ft. Ridgely, beaten about the head with a violin case until her face was an unrecognizable mush, then seized by the feet and smashed against a wagon wheel again and again before being hurled to the hysterical mother. Her other daughter, an infant, was hacked to pieces before her eyes with a tomahawk, then she, too, hurled to the mother, who had collapsed on an old mattress taken from the wagon. Then the mattress, with Mrs. Henderson and the bodies of the two children, was thrown into a huge inferno and consumed in the flames.

The killers' rage was not confined to the settlers. With their natural animosities shored up by gallons of stolen whiskey and the ease of the "victories" they had secured over their unarmed victims, the invaders turned their attention to the half-breeds and "cut-hair" Indians they felt were leading their people to become as the white oppressors. But the cut-hairs, for the most part, were former members of the warrior class, and responded to threats of violence with threats of their own. From the beginning, there were splits in the ranks of the raiders. It wasn't the "Indians" who were responsible for the carnage, but largely the work of one segment, the Mdewakanton traditionals, who initiated the slaughter before having time to recruit other local bands of the Santee nation.

Other groups did come in during the next couple of days, when the ferocity of the attacks and the element of surprise left the momentary impression that the attackers actually were gaining the upper hand. The roadblocks put up by the cut-hairs and others not involved in the attacks did little to impress the killers, but they did annoy therm. Frustrated by targeted victims willing to put up a fight, the raiders went instead with renewed vengeance against those unwilling or unable to, and the bloodletting spread like a dry-grass prairie fire.

The road between the Agency and Fort Ridgely, was hardly a road at all, but a wide trail marked by twin ruts of grass kept matted by the occasional passage of iron-clad wagon wheels and just barely visible enough in the dark to keep travelers from getting lost. It was, luckily enough, a familiar conduit to safety, since virtually all whites at the Agency had to have come through the fort first. It was along this road, now, that the stream of terrified refugees began to flee. Unfortunately, the attackers were equally familiar with the road, and had no interest in permitting the survivors to alert the troops. Many were killed as they fled by warriors who simply hid behind trees, waiting for their quarry to pass. Even then the relationship between red and white had been sufficiently familiar that the assassins could simply approach with upraised palm, offering to "protect" the victim, which they did until driving their hatchets into a turned back, or gutting some quaking lass with a shotgun blast to the abdomen.

By the end of the first day, at least 31 mutilated bodies lay rotting on the damp soil of the Minnesota River bluffs.

CHAPTER TWENTY THREE

Around 10:00 AM that morning, August 18th, the relative calm of the fort was shattered by the sounds of lash on horseflesh and the violent creaking of wagon wheels as a buckboard careened through the ring of outer buildings onto the relative protection of the Ft. Ridgely parade ground. The wagon contained the driver, who operated the boarding house at the Lower Agency, his family, and four terrified Agency workers, two of whom were Sioux women.

The driver, J.C.Dickenson, was a quiet and introspective innkeeper turned madman. He sawed on the reins and yanked on the wheel brake until he scraped to a halt before the Fort's stone barracks.

"Help!", he screamed. "We're dying! They're loose! We're all cut up!" Leaving his dazed passengers in the wagon, the driver, wearing only a pair of suspendered trousers with neither shirt nor boots, leaped from his seat and scurried to all corners of the parade ground, red-faced, yelling for help, finally dropping to his knees and clutching, sobbing, at the base of the post flagpole.

Aroused by the man's dramatic arrival, Captain Marsh had emerged from his office, clamping his hat on his head. Assigning an orderly to look after the wagon's passengers, he beckoned to boyish, 19-year-old Lt.Thomas Gere, and ran to where the driver was now sitting on the muddy soil.

"The Indians have broken out", Dickenson gasped. "They're slaughtering every white soul at the agency. Andrew Myrick is dead. Peter Asbury is dead, his nose cut off. The two Berger girls were hauled to the woods without clothes. Torgerson's head has been chopped right off! The Miller baby is impaled to a tree with a hatchet. There must be a hundred of the murdering devils! They've gone mad!"

Captain Marsh did his best to calm the discourse, at least to the point of getting an accurate report. He took Dickenson aside, and sat with him for several minutes, then sent the man to unhitch his horses to give him something to do. Then the women were questioned. They confirmed the tales of brutality and murder they had witnessed, giving the names of the perpetrators they knew. The Indian women gave a less emotional report, ashamed, frightened at what might await them at the hands of the whites. Yesterday they were friends. Today, they were sure, they were counted among the enemy.

Captain John S. Marsh was 29 years old, regular army, not a volunteer. He was a large man, a beefy six feet, and accustomed to the respect of other men. He had been tested in combat at the first Battle of Bull Run, and had emerged unhurt and confident of his ability as both a fighter and a leader. He had fared well, he thought, in previous discourses with Sioux headmen. He had calmed the situation at the annuity distribution site just weeks earlier, and had felt that he had earned the respect of the native leaders. He had, on many occasions, spoken personally with Little Crow.

But John Marsh was also something of a bigot, comfortable with what he saw as the natural superiority of the white race. While he relished the respect of what he saw as his charges, he granted them virtually none in return. They were weak, and Captain Marsh had no tolerance for weakness. While horrified at the turn of events before him, he could barely bring himself to believe that the Dakota elders with whom he had treated would be rash enough to challenge the might of the

United States Military – and he as its representative – nor to choke off all support from the government.

No. The Captain was a decisive man, and he had already made up his mind. Mr. Dickenson had said there must have been a hundred of them. He accepted that – a small rogue band from among the six thousand still waiting for their annuity payment. And they had wreaked havoc on an untrained and largely unarmed population. Though he would be outnumbered, he would see how those savages stacked up against a well-armed punitive force with superior planning, adequate ammunition and a rage to equal that of the murderers themselves.

"Lt. Gere!", he shouted, though the young officer was but arm's length away. "I want volunteers. You will remain with a small force here. Do not leave the fort unprotected. Provide two extra rations of ammunition per man, and have the volunteers formed up here in one hour. Dismissed!".

Interpreter Quinn stood by the Captain as he issued his order. He, too, felt the rage swelling up within him, but his assessment differed in almost every respect from that of his forceful commander. After 35 years in residence with the Sioux, he had an almost instinctive understanding not of *what* they thought, but *how*. He had been with the groups of Dakota leaders on their treaty treks to Washington. He saw what they saw, and conversed with them regarding the limitless power of the Great Father and the whites who had come to dot the prairies much like the Bison of old. The leaders, he knew, had largely been able to suppress their own frustrations, and accept the inevitability of terms dictated by a clearly superior power. This was not the work of those elders. And if the elders had been overridden then the cork was out of the bottle. Without the proud memories of the old, the young had endured what they felt was a system of semi-slavery since birth. Only the tempering influence of those accepted as wiser had kept them from breaking those bonds. With that influence gone, God help us, he thought, as he turned to secure his weapons.

    Captain Marsh's senses were acutely-tuned as he contemplated his next steps. In the next half-hour, three more parties of settlers charged into the parade ground in unleashed panic, many suffering from wounds, others, sure they were being followed, racing to seek shelter in the stone barracks building. In each case, the escapees emphasized how general the uprising appeared to be, and how many "hundreds" of warriors appeared to be taking part. This was not what Marsh wanted to hear – so he didn't. In motion now, he strode to his quarters, arming himself not only with rifle and saber, but his own Colt revolver and a bone-handled Bowie knife that had been for him one of the spoils of war at Bull Run. He felt fully confident to handle the situation, but followed military procedure by dispatching an urgent request to Lt. Sheehan as he and his troop wended their way back to Ft. Ripley:

> *Headquarters, Fort Ridgely*
> *August 18, 1862*
> *Lieut Sheehan*
>   *It is absolutely necessary that you should return with your command immediately to this post. The Indians are raising hell at the Lower Agency. Return as soon as possible.*
>   *John S. Marsh*
>   Capt Commd Post

CHAPTER TWENTY FOUR

Within 90 minutes of the arrival of the first survivors, Captain Marsh, 46 troopers and interpreter Quinn were on the road to the now-burning agency. They had each been issued 40 rounds of ammunition, and a single day's rations. There were no bugles, no flapping guidons. Marsh and Quinn were mounted on mules for the 11-mile journey, the troops on foot at double-time for most of the first three miles. Then the transportation Marsh ordered finally caught up, and the men scrambled into the awkward caravan of buckboards and hay wagons that was to take them to what was to be for many their first and last battle.

Six miles out from the fort the troop began to see dead and mutilated bodies by the side of the narrow road. Only one was armed. There were four women, a toddler and an infant – a baby girl - among them. The toddler's arm lay at an awkward angle, broken. The infant, though her stomach was sliced open, was somehow still alive. The men moved grimly on. Moments later a party of refugees led by the Rev. Samuel Hinman, Episcopal missionary and pastor to Little Crow only the previous morning, came into view, sobbing and grasping at the men they saw as their saviors. Marsh informed the Reverend of the infant back up the road. Hinman informed Marsh that the Captain was badly outnumbered, and begged him to save his men and turn around.

"And then what of the others?", Marsh inquired angrily. "What will become of them?".

"It has already become of them", the minister responded with a barely audible voice. "All who are living are here".

Marsh ended the conversation with the boast that he had enough powder and lead to whip every Indian between there and the Pacific Ocean.

Coming up to the two, Quinn – whose instincts for danger were much more finely tuned than Marsh's - supported caution as well. His own goodbyes at the fort had been more extended and emotional than usual. His manner now was gloomy, on edge. Though a civilian, he would follow his commanding officer, though he felt the young officer was being reckless in his assessment, and his willingness to throw the lives of 46 troopers at the avalanche of mayhem that was clearly before them.

For a moment, the arguments of the Reverend and his interpreter appeared to be swaying the Captain, who paused long enough in his outpouring of bravado to look back at his men, and the victims arrayed before him. But ultimately, the sight of the dazed survivors, and the mutilated, still warm bodies in the ditches by the road, filled him with an even greater resolve. These were the acts of ravenous *cowards*! Assigning two of his force to accompany the Reverend and his meager flock back to the fort, and still harboring the notion that the sight of his handful of blue uniforms would set the cowards scurrying, Marsh excused himself and set off with a grim new mindset. Starting off as a commander seeking justice, he had evolved into a warrior seeking vengeance. It was now personal. He waved his wagons forward.

To reach the Lower Sioux Agency, the detachment had to traverse the primitive road to the Redwood Ferry, the means by which all travelers had to cross the Minnesota River. Moments after leaving Rev. Hinman, the troop reached Faribault Hill, where the road descended into a broad river bottom with tall grass and massive cottonwoods lining both sides of the river itself.

Warning his teamsters to mind their brakes on the hill, Marsh motioned the troop to continue.

"Be alert now", he gruffly cautioned.

He was a young man, but an old-fashioned soldier. He adhered to a rigid code of honor, and expected the same of those with whom he came into contact. You looked people in the eye. You kept your word. You shared danger without complaint. You exhibited valor in battle, but gave quarter when asked. Winning the *war* was the goal, in order to preserve the principles being defended. Individual battles were secondary. But if combat were necessary, let it be face-to-face, and let the better man win. John Marsh believed in the *nobility* of war.

The wild-eyed warriors of Taoyateduta did not.

CHAPTER TWENTY FIVE

It was too still. Even in the throes of his righteous anger, Captain Marsh's emotional insulation wasn't enough to blind him to the precarious nature of his current position. As he led his troops along the riverside trail, the lushness of the surrounding vegetation grew progressively richer, darker. The troop had been walking along the level for some time now. No more survivors were met. There were no sounds of activity of any sort – except for the whispers of his men, the creaking of their wagons and the occasional snort from one of the mules.

Less than a half-mile from the ferry, Marsh suddenly dismounted, and ordered Quinn to do the same. Lower profile target, he mused, though aware of sacrificing visibility for purposes of command.

The surrounding growth was now almost oppressive. It was simply impossible to see more than several feet into it. Marsh now wished he had placed less emphasis on warriors fighting "fairly", and had put skirmishers out to smoke out the enemy before his entire troop got into a situation they might not readily emerge from.

He sent whispered orders for all to dismount, and the teamsters to take the wagons to the rear. Less noise, less concentration of targets. He ordered silence among the men, and to proceed single file with no less than four paces between. Then he reconnoitered by ear. Surely, less than a mile from the Agency, and part of that the glassy echo chamber of the river, he would be able to pick up *some* of the sounds of destruction. Nothing more than the natural pulse of the bottoms – birds, a scampering squirrel, the delicate hiss of the river itself as it flowed placidly by. He signaled his men forward.

They were wary, wide-eyed. Many had not known the full nature of the mission until meeting Rev. Hinman, and still carried with them the horror of what they saw, and the Reverend's hearfelt warnings to return. They were young farmers and clerks, most barely past their mid-teens, virtually none of whom had ever fired at anything that might fire back. Marsh damned the southern war now for taking all the seasoned troops. And he damned the Indians for needing them. He shouldn't be here. But he couldn't *not* be here.

The file advanced without speaking, glancing to all sides, trying to pierce the darkness that lined their grassy corridor.

"Halt!", a raspy whisper commanded. "Who's there?".

Precious Jesus save us, Marsh thought, not for what might have been seen, but for the command that had broken their silence. Silence? That, too, what a myth, Marsh knew, still clinging to the possibility that the primitive raiders might have fled the sounds of his "superior force". Hurrying to the source of the muffled outburst about a third of the way back up the file, he came across a pair of unharmed civilians who had just stepped from the forest to reveal themselves to the passing troops. One proved to be a trembling John Humphrey. The other was Cyrus Magner, owner of a vegetable patch on which was the lean-to once occupied by Humphrey's family. He had been approaching from the river to investigate the sounds heard from the agency, and had run into the fleeing boy. Both of them had been holed up for hours, waiting for darkness to fall before heading to the fort.

Marsh was torn. The boy told of what he'd heard, and that he was certain of his family's death. But maybe, *maybe,* someone still lived. Would the Captain escort them just the quarter of a mile or so to the site of the lean-to? Marsh asked if they'd heard sounds of the Indians while they hid. Voices on the other side of the river, Magner said, nothing on this side. They couldn't make out if they were Indian or white.

Perhaps relieved to postpone what they now saw as an inevitable clash with the Sioux raiders, Marsh and the troop made their way slowly up the hill to Magner's lean-to. It provided a scene of utter horror to survivor and soldier alike. The lean-to itself, sturdy enough to have been a livable cabin minus a couple of walls, had been set ablaze, arm-sized glowing embers now nearly covering the bodies of the boy's mother, father, brother and sister. The smoke and smell of burning flesh, the literal sizzle of it, emptied the bellies of two of the Captain's troopers. The clothing of both the women had been ripped partially off, the mother's mouth locked agape in a soundless scream, her arched neck bruised and broken. John's sister appeared to be alive, sitting at the base of a tree. But she had been pinned to the tree with a spear, and had, mercifully, long since died there. The boy, face down in the ash, had been scalped. In front of the lean-to, down a slight slope, his father lay backwards across a fallen log, a bullet in his forehead, his throat slit, a small hatchet still clutched tightly in his right hand.

There was little that could be done. Sobbing, young John begged for at least a proper burial for his family members, but Marsh wisely refused, having already lost, he was sure, any element of surprise that would provide favor in the conflict to come. He promised to complete the task later, though, and detailed a pair of privates to escort the two civilians back to the crest of Faribault Hill. Then Marsh and his men removed the deceased to a thicket and covered their bodies with foliage until their return.

    The side journey had been a horrible experience for the green troops, but beneficial to their mission. Those who had been as yet unconvinced of the barbarity of their enemy now saw them in a more realistic light. Some who had harbored more fear than anger had those emotions firmly reversed. Glances were exchanged, silent prayers said, ammunition packs checked. As a unit, the resolve to exact revenge on what they saw as a renegade band of baby-killers what now palpable. Their timid steps of less than an hour ago were replaced with the controlled but purposeful strides of men eager to mete out their own justice.

    200 feet east of the landing, on the north side of the road, the troop encountered the stone cabin normally occupied by the ferryman. Taking no chances, Captain Marsh ordered the main force of his company to step off the trail into the woods while interpreter Quinn, a sergeant and a half-dozen troopers approached the structure from the best cover available. Motioning one of the privates toward the single window overlooking the river, Quinn snuck to the door from the opposite side, bursting into the cabin with a burly shoulder to the heavy plank door, tearing it free from one of its weathered leather hinges. The noise of the assault echoed clearly back up the trail, bringing most of the men back to the road in a rush. The stone hut, however, was empty, containing but a bunk, a 3-legged table propped up partially with milk crates, a stool and a spilled bowl of oatmeal.

    Concerned about the noise but with a growing confidence that he was chasing a cowardly band fleeing the retribution of the United States military, Marsh allowed the men to advance past the cabin to the river clearing while he, Quinn and the sergeant plotted their next move. The field of view here was limited, with thickets of hazel and willow mingled with waist-high bear grass on both sides of the road. Across the river, the high bluffs that hid the Redwood Agency tilted precipitously toward the river, their lower face covered with trees and underbrush.

"Hell of a place for an ambush", the experienced interpreter muttered to the young Captain, nodding toward the tight congregation of blue uniforms now migrating toward the river's pastoral banks.

Marsh nodded, saying nothing.

"Captain!", a corporal hissed from his perch on a river stump. "We've got company!".

Heads snapped in unison as the troopers froze momentarily at the pronouncement, then, unable to pick up the alleged visitors at first glance, dove for whatever cover they could find.

A single Indian emerged from the thicket across the river, and stood for a moment with his arms raised, as if assuring the frightened young Americans they need not concern themselves so. Quinn squinted, then identified the figure to Captain Marsh as White Dog, a cut-hair farmer Indian who had seemed content in adopting the ways of the white man. He was also a gambler, and to the interpreter's certain knowledge, a cheat. His words were now soothing and fatherly in tone.

"Come across", he said. "Everything is right over here. We do not want to fight. There will be no trouble. Come over to the Agency and we will hold a council".

"You bet your ass we'll hold a council!" Quinn growled in return. "I'll be right here on this log. *You* come over – and bring your band there in the grass with you."

White Dog said nothing, but shrugged his shoulders and held out his hands as if to question Quinn's distrustful response. For several minutes there was silence, Marsh's troops rigid save for swiveling heads, White Dog statue-like, as if dominating the closing scene of a stage play.

Captain Marsh knew the Sioux farmer to be among the "friendlies" at the agency, one who had even been a voice of moderation at the recent stand-off at the warehouse. Still believing that his opponents were a small force of renegades, even now fleeing toward the west, Marsh decided to cross over and recruit White Dog and his group to assist in capturing and killing the outlaw band. Never questioning why the Sioux would keep his companions hidden, a fact confirmed by two troopers who had spied the lurking Indians while relieving themselves downstream from the clearing, Marsh ordered the ferry prepared for crossing. An agitated Sergeant John Bishop then approached the Captain with more sightings of hidden warriors, these on *this* side of the river. They were surrounded. Still White Dog stood, now with shotgun by his side, as if a primitive soldier at a mocking version of parade rest.

Concerned now, Marsh order his men to line up at the river in alternating positions, effectively creating a long oval of armed men facing outwards, covering the clearings and undergrowth on both sides of the river. Though they were totally exposed, seeking cover in the dense foliage now occupied by the enemy would prove even more potentially disastrous, he felt. He moved among the men, directing lines of fire, reassuring the obviously nervous ones. Under other circumstances, it would have presented a formidable sight, nearly 50 armed men defending a single position. It was also a standoff. If the cowardly renegades were fleeing, who was surrounding him? Had the entire tribe supported this uprising?

With Little Crow's expression of support, the tribe, in effect, had *become* the renegades. While the befuddled Captain weighed his options, upwards of 300 seething Sioux warriors, elders and cut-hairs as well as the young, crept closer to the fidgety bluecoats, trembling themselves at the opportunity to crush these symbols of white oppression.

Occasionally a leaf would rattle, or a twig snap. Squirrels snap small twigs, Quinn knew. These were big twigs. And the breaking sounds were closer, more now on their side of the river.

Like two curs circling one another seeking that first opening, the sides prepared. The captain sent a whispered message, and within a minute all of his troops had gone to kneeling or prone positions, ammo bags opened and accessible. Personal hunting knives appeared out of rucksacks, and were placed before their owners. Rifles were now at the troopers' shoulders, scanning the trees, waiting for a charge, a shouted order, *something.*

An even worse outcome may have followed had the warriors been given time to close up their ring on the defenders, but the plan was foiled by the nerves of White Dog himself, who suddenly picked up his shotgun, discharged both booming barrels, and hurled himself behind the protection of a massive Cottonwood log. He had been aiming at the defiant figure of Mr. Quinn, but knowing that raising the shotgun to his shoulder would have brought instant death, had fired from the waist.

Quinn, having twitched with the Indian's move, was struck by no more than a half-dozen pellets, all embedded in the greasy leather leggings he customarily wore when outside the fort.

The interpreter's roar of "Fuck you!" achieved nearly the volume of White Dog's hand-cannon, but his need to vent proved his downfall, making him the target of choice for the now-standing band of attackers stretching nearly out of sight both upstream and down. No fewer than a dozen pellets and slugs riddled the hide of the grizzled frontiersman as he jerked this way and that in a macabre dance under the fusillade, and plunged face-first into the muddy river.

The bullets buzzed like angry hornets from that point, rifles on both sides spewing puffs of smoke that hung like dirty oversized cotton balls in the still air. At first, the soldiers concentrated their fire across the river, desperate to avenge the slaughter of the popular father-figure. This but for seconds, until troopers at the perimeter of the now-massed blue uniforms began to shriek and tumble over where they knelt. They *were* surrounded.

"Perimeter out, perimeter out!", Marsh screamed, there being no standard military order for this situation. Immediately the soldiers on the eastern edge of the clearing turned east to face their hidden enemy, prostrating themselves behind clumps of bear grass and the few trees scattered within the clearing. The staccato burst of rifle and shotgun fire echoed down the river bed, dissipating at the next bend. No help would be coming from that direction for the beleaguered troop.

John Marsh stood boldly in the center of the melee, the onslaught too sudden for fear. His first instinct was to mass his firepower for an overwhelming counterattack to open an avenue of escape – but *where?*

At whom? His assailants had melted back into the undergrowth. They were truly cowards, with not even the courage to step out behind their shelter and trade fire like men. Miraculously unscathed by the balls whizzing by him, the bold young officer dropped to one knee, ordering his men to keep down, to conserve ammunition, and to return fire through the center of the smoky discharges now so numerous as to nearly engulf the small band of troopers.

Private Reginald Quary hunkered down in the tall grass at the river's edge. Eyeing the movement of braves on the opposite shore through the Captain's binoculars he'd salvaged from the dust when they all dove for cover, he noted a formation of large branches about sixty yards upstream, floating toward the site of the ambush. At first he paid little attention, trying to restore movement in the fingers of his wounded trigger hand. Then he noticed the bright green, fresh, leaves on the branches.

"Captain! Redskins in the water!", he screamed, pointing toward the heads now barely visible behind the jumbled floating foliage. Somehow, Marsh was able to separate a pair of sharpshooters from the general conflagration, and position them upstream of the main battle. The marauders, at a disadvantage from their need to stay concealed, their weapons notched in the limbs of branches to stay dry, proved sitting ducks for the riflemen. Two were killed with the first volley, two more wounded. The wounded and two more unhurt quickly abandoned their float, hurled their weapons to the opposite side of the narrow river, and followed with strokes born of fear for life. One more of their number was felled as he climbed from the water and gestured violently at the still-engaged sharpshooters.

"One more for you, Mr. Quinn", whispered the observer Quary.

No longer was there any illusion on the part of Captain Marsh that they were going to "punish" the Indians. The goal now was survival. The difference in visual perception was remarkable. Coming in, assured of victory, little was really noticed of the surrounding territory – places for ambush, routes for escape – because they didn't *have* to be. Projected victory insulates the observer, brings comfort to the moment. Now there was no projected victory, no comfort whatsoever. Now every snapped twig, every break in the undercover, every point of access to the riverbank burst on the visual field of every man for whom each of those things had become critical to the maintenance of life itself. Captain Marsh's mind had been focused. Now it whirled. Could *this* help? *That?* His mind instinctively sought out elements of *hope,* no matter their form.

Realizing finally the indefensibility of their position, he sought hope in an immediate retreat to the only structure in the area, the ferry house. He didn't stop to think about the capacity of that tiny building. It had *walls*. Word was passed that the soldiers gradually work their way to a smaller clearing within sight of the stone cabin. Using effective covering fire and sticking to the cover of the woods, the troopers – those yet unscathed and the walking wounded – converged on the clearing within a several-minute span. Seven were missing, and no one volunteered to return for them. After reports on their fate were assessed, and injuries and weapons checked, Marsh formed his troops, rasped "Now", and set off at a crouching run to the only possible port of safety for his faltering command.

But the Sioux had proven the masters of military strategy this day. As the frightened troops retreated to their only shelter, several previously uncommitted warriors dropped out of the *trees* surrounding the cabin, while a grotesquely-painted handful poured forth from the structure itself. To their credit, the inexperienced volunteers did not panic, but hit the ground or sought cover behind rocks or trees, and returned fire nearly as hot as that they got from the native force both before and behind them.

The firing lasted for more than an hour, scouring the trees and leaving a pall of smoke, a grimy, acrid, low-hanging cloud that blinded the eye and assaulted the lung.

Several of the younger warriors attempted at first to count coup on the green troopers, but were shot through by squirrel-shooters who felt no similar need to broadcast their own fearlessness. A number of hand-to-hand contests were conducted, most ending with the attacker being shot from point-blank range by a nearby trooper. Both sides expended so much ammunition that the firing had been reduced to sporadic volleys and sniping, though the warriors had the advantage of bows not employed earlier in the ambush. Corporal David Siegal, a valiant and popular trooper married less than a week, was shot clear through the base of the neck with an arrow. He dropped his weapon and ran through the line for almost fifty feet before collapsing face first into a bramble. He had died when hit, his spinal cord severed. He'd run on reflex alone, like a beheaded chicken. The scene did little to shore up the courage of the remaining soldiers, though they had come through the previous hour with no dead, and but four wounded.

All said and done, it was the obscured vision produced by the cloud of powder smoke that kept the volunteer force from being totally annihilated.

In the brief span of the battle, John Marsh had been transformed from a noble defender of the downtrodden to a grimy, tear-streaked commander whose leadership abilities had been tried – and convicted. Later reports indicated that "scores of Indians lay dead", to be sure, but this was not a contest, to be scored. His own ranks had been severely thinned. Men depending on his foresight and battle wisdom had been brutally and unnecessarily killed. He had had to defend the white population, but not by plunging into a natural ambush by what had been described as a vastly superior force because he allowed his emotion to overpower his common sense and command responsibilities. The troops that remained were supporting nearly a dozen wounded, many badly. They had no food, little ammunition, and were completely surrounded by a superior enemy. The prognosis was grim, and though his intentions were heroic, his behavior on this day was not.

And the young captain knew it. For the first time since the initial load of survivors clattered into the fort, John Marsh took a realistic inventory of his situation, and focused on equally realistic options. There were few. Though he was unable to *count* his adversaries, their-now free movements through the brush, the volume of muzzle flashes, and flow of red warriors over the agency bluffs left no doubt that he was severely outnumbered on all sides.

He had but one factor in his favor. Due in part to their limited numbers and the felt value of each man, red men of all tribes generally fought more cautiously than the traditional battle tactic of the white – to throw in all available manpower in an effort to overwhelm an enemy, casualties be damned. The native typically employed harassing tactics, going for the kill when the risk of *being* killed was low. Head-on assaults on fully-armed opponents were rare, frequently tapering off when the element of surprise was no longer theirs. Such was the case at the moment. Though badly outnumbered, the white soldiers did not crumble as they were expected to do. While many of their number lay dead, the warriors had paid for those deaths with more than one of their own for each white, and the whites had withstood several all-out assaults, and still had ammunition. The slaughter had been easy at first, and there were still towns to be raided, goods to be taken, and women to be used. Was this worth the price being paid?

The questions were not being asked by a leader. This raiding party, as most at first, had no leader. The killings were in the nature of crazed celebrations, all equal, all glorying in the vengeance of their actions. Who to say "stay", and who to move on?

John Marsh had no way of estimating the mindset of his attackers, and spent no time seeking it. The potential for reinforcements was nil, he knew. Lt. Gere had been left with barely a skeleton force; they would be fully occupied treating – and defending, if necessary – the stream of survivors he knew would be descending on the fort. Marsh by now felt that it was possible that the whole Sioux nation had risen up, and may have planned attacks on multiple fronts. He no longer thought of them as unthinking primitives, but canny adversaries bent on massive destruction. God save Gere and his survivors if they were attacked in what was laughingly described as a "fort". A fort without walls? Come in, please? He thought of the dispatch sent to Lt. Sheehan, but he knew Sheehan's command had to be at least 40 miles from Ft. Ridgely by the time the courier got to it, then the return, on foot? No help. No. There had been no attacks for the previous hour. Maybe the raiders had been called off by someone who had emerged as leader? He'd seen several climbing *up* the bluff. Were they having a council to determine how to best wipe out his force?

He saw hesitation on the part of the enemy, and limited visibility provided by both underbrush and lingering smoke, and determined that now was the time to move. He knew that the dense tangle by the river continued for several miles toward the fort, and sent a scout to reconnoiter that direction, and another to move toward the big clearing to determine if there were any survivors, and if they could be moved. Twenty minutes later, both scouts had returned, one with two badly wounded but mobile survivors, the other with the news that troops could *hide* as they passed through the bushes by the river, but that it would be bushwacking all the way.

In between the road and the river were roughly 90 yards of trees, grasses and brambly underbrush thick enough to hide a man a half-dozen yards away. This visual advantage proved a terrible drain, however, on men who had endured what these had over the past 12 hours. They were exhausted, terrified, many suffering from debilitating wounds, some shell-shocked and unable to move save for specific orders from their commander. And those orders came in the form of whispered rasps from man to man; spread out; move toward the river; keep low; don't fire unless you're sure of your target.

Like rivulets of sweat down a craggy face, the ragged band of survivors oozed as silently as possible toward the fort, over brambles and fallen logs, around clearings, into the river itself when the brush became too thick to traverse. Two of the men were no longer able to walk. One hobbled, clinging to a pole stretching between the shoulders of two of the ablebodied, the other laying on a rough litter made of branches and uniform shirts. The temperature was in the low 90s now, mosquitoes forming in clouds. One hour. Two hours. Only spotty firing, now, but warriors spotted on the road, walking easily, pointing, hurling insults and threats.

    The soldier band had stopped long enough for stragglers to catch up when word came back from the scouts. The thicket ended 200 yards further on, converting to marsh grasses with no trees whatsoever. At least 30 braves were visible, waiting. Marsh agonized once again. Would a massed charge break through the assailants? He ordered the men to place all their extra ammunition into a passed hat, then redistributed the meager supply. Each man wound up with five rounds. A massed charge might get them another half-mile, but with at least five miles to go to the fort, it would be a suicide mission. Better to withstand a siege in the brush; the Dakota knew neither the number of troopers surviving, nor the size of their ammo supply, and seemed reluctant to charge blindly into what could be withering fire. They rested; scouts out on all sides.

    Private Jeremiah Doolittle, a diminutive young man with an irrepressible spirit, approached Captain Marsh as the dusk was settling. Look, he whispered. The trail on the opposite side of the river had ascended onto high bluffs. No Indian movement had been noted for nearly a half-hour. Could it be that those following across the river had decided to leave the slaughter to the hundreds already on this side? Could they have gone after other "game"? Marsh followed the youngster to the shore. It was almost dark, but through the glasses he could confirm Doolittle's assessment. There was no movement, no evidence of danger. There would be no *reason* for the braves to remain hidden if they were there. The risk, of course, was present, but the Captain's military training had included the need for rapid evaluation and decision-making. The risks of a crossing were considerably less than those of charging almost unarmed into a band of Sioux warriors bristling with weapons and gone obviously mad. Darkness would be their benefactor; they would cross.

The firing at this hour was minimal. Some of the men were down to one or two rounds. Almost all pledged to use them only at point-blank range or, if they were overrun, on each other. Marsh summoned the remaining sergeant, John Bishop, and the two surviving corporals, and informed them of his intention to cross. The river was narrow at this point, deceptively so. It looked to be no more than 25 yards across, but part of that was illusion, the thick foliage on the other bank being reflected back into the water and appearing in the dusk to be solid land. The river was, in fact, close to double that width. Probes did indicate that it was shallow, perhaps only waist-deep. Marsh, in spite of not being a swimmer, elected to be the first to cross. If there was risk, whether of drowning or enemy fire, he had no hesitation at this point to assume it; it was his leadership that had put them in this position. Removing his saber belt and holding it and his rifle above his head, he looked around once, and waded determinedly into the river.

Two factors combined to affect his crossing. The first was the current. While the river was narrower here than at other points, compressing a body of flowing water into a smaller space necessarily speeds up that flow. The low light and lack of wind produced a calm surface that belied the velocity beneath it. The second was the tendency of the faster-flowing water to gouge out the muddy bottom to accommodate its flow. As Captain Marsh plowed through the muck, he encountered a steep slope in the center of the river, and slid down its edge until the water reached eye-level. Struggling to maintain his balance while keeping his weapons extended above the water line, he lost his footing altogether and slid beneath the fast-flowing surface. There was no outcry, but Sergeant Bishop, crab-walking beside the column to ensure all got across, saw Marsh's fall and growled a soft order to "Get him!". As if they had practiced the move, the next two troopers in line passed their rifles back down the line, and plunged beneath the water, desperate to find their captain, but without alerting the enemy to their watery route. But the Captain remained submerged. When his body was recovered days later, he was still clutching his sword and rifle.

Bishop guided the rest of the men – now numbering less than half the original force – across to a mucky but flat shoreline. Once across, most literally collapsed. For several minutes there was silence, then a murmured confirmation that all except the Captain had made the crossing. This was a time for fear, and it surfaced in the majority of them. Signs of the Cross were heard, as were prayers, curses and tears. Until then, they had been in combat, adrenalin supporting whatever courage they could muster. Now, apparently trapped, with unknown hordes of savage enemy pressing in on them with few tools to resist, their fate rose in their throats. They had seen how the end had come to others, and had no reason to expect it would be different with them.

Hopelessness, however, produces its own energy. With nothing to lose, and guided by the now urgent commands of Sgt. Bishop, the survivors clung to the shoreline of the river itself in silent, single-file caravan, moving through the muck but barely a mile each hour, thankful for the moonless night but certain of their death around each curve. Nearly six hours into their muddy ordeal, long past the peak of Faribault Hill, Bishop sent out scouts who determined to their disbelief that the band was no longer being followed.

Ravaged by their ordeal, boots sloshing, clothing torn, exposed skin paved with mosquito bites, the group made its way to the road and an hour later stumbled into the quagmire that had become Ft.Ridgely. Of the 47 men who embarked on the ill-fated venture, 14 in this group came straggling back this day, and eight more the following. The rest were lost to the "renegade band" of Mdewakanton Sioux who even now had begun spreading terror throughout the counties of southern Minnesota.

The outcome of Captain Marsh's clash had never been in doubt. Little Crow's force at the ferry landing was later found to exceed 300 from the lower agency, 25 from the upper band, and another 25 Winnebagoes. The plan had been to lure Marsh's troops onto the ferry, then cut the rope and massacre the lot from both sides as they floated down the river. The plan was foiled by White Dog's nerves, but given the disparity in force size, Marsh's troops were seen as having performed well and, in individual cases, heroically.

There are those who later said that the captain should have taken the advice of Rev. Hinman and turned back to the fort with him. Such opinions were greatly disputed by others. No man of courage, no leader of a troop with the potential to stop slaughter would turn about in the face of that slaughter, leaving its victims in his wake. Sgt. Bishop opined that such a man should himself be shot. In a later review, he also said:

"Moreover, if we had returned to the fort at once, the band of Indians would certainly have followed us in hot pursuit, and would undoubtedly have captured the fort that night, and there would have been nothing to stop them until they reached Ft. Snelling"

CHAPTER TWENTY SIX

Sheehan's return to Ft. Ridgely at Marsh's urging was an effort of will by his entire troop. He had read the dispatch as signifying emergency and removed all stops to meet it.

The speed of his return was achieved in spite of several brief stops to administer to the wounded they encountered along the way. These were people who had gone *beyond* the fort in their panic to put distance between themselves and the marauding natives. One man lay on his side in a wagon, an arrow entering his lower belly and protruding a half a foot higher in back. An elderly lady had had her breast practically cleaved off with a knife. A young child, a boy of no more than 6 or 7, had been half-scalped by the heathens, the hair and flesh on the right side of his head practically all removed, he, open-mouthed, weakly waving at the cloud of flies fighting to settle on the oozing wound. Practically all the wounded were in a state of shock, few able to speak at all, some whose jaws continued to work though no sound came out. Those not bleeding would all try to speak at once, shouting above each other to give the most detailed descriptions of what had happened to them and give out the names – they all knew the names – of their attackers.

As if not sufficiently motivated, the troops received yet another dispatch some 20 minutes after leaving their last aid stop. This one, from Lt. Gere, was more descriptive:

Force your march returning. Captain Marsh and most of his command were killed yesterday at the Lower Agency. Little Crow and about 600 Sioux warriors are now approaching the fort and will undoubtedly attack us. *About 250 refugees have arrived here for protection. Return as quickly as a merciful God will permit you.*

For the last several miles to the fort the troop alternately trotted and walked in their stocking feet, boots and any heavy items other than firearms having been stored in one of the two mule-drawn wagons accompanying the soldiers.

No mercy had been shown on the road to Ft. Ridgely, nor from it. Those who did survive did so not just at the direction of a merciful God. The rage of the Sioux warriors was directed not solely at the *person* of the whites, but the *things* that sustained him, and had for long memory been denied the Indian. The attacks at this stage were spur-of-the-moment outbursts. Taoyeduta's capitulation had granted the *when* of the uprising, but not the *how*, and while the taste of blood was now fresh in the minds of the marauders, the things that were now available for the taking were irresistible, and often diverted the killers from their intended mayhem.

Sheehan's troops had been marching through the rain all night. The noise of their own movement prevented them from hearing the first stirrings of the fort as they approached, leaving the initial sighting of the reinforcements to one of the post's outlying sentries – who violated all military decorum by firing his rifle into the air and screaming without pause that troops had arrived.

The effect of their arrival was immediate and dramatic on both rescued and rescuers. Having walked over 40 miles, most in the dark of night, in under 10 hours, Sheehan's troops had the appearance of men who had been consistently flogged - heads down, shoulders slumped, stumbling, expressionless. With the uproar that emerged from the fort, their backs straightened, eyes brightened, their pace quickened as if fresh from a night's rest. Seeing that the fort was not at that moment under siege let the rescuers think, if only momentarily, that there need be no life-and-death battle here today. The morale of the moment was high and climbing.

From the fort's side, the appearance of – how many, 20? 50? 100? – blue uniforms meant, of course, instant survival. It had been a nightmare, but now it was light. This was tomorrow. The nightmare was over. God *bless* these saviors! Their arrival turned a scene of mortal despair into one of joyous bedlam. Sighted more than a half-mile from the fort, the soldiers were granted a welcome as boisterous as any politician's rally, the raucous, back-slapping greeting serving to at least temporarily dispel the sheer physical exhaustion felt by all parties. This went on for nearly an hour, with neither officer attempting to restrict the celebration. To one another, however, Sheehan and Gere spoke reality.

>*Tuesday, August 19*
>*Assumed command at Fort Ridgely commenced fortifying garrison Inds were approaching garrison ordered the gunner to go shelling them immediately which kept them off all day. On consultation with Mr. Waycoff of the Indian department – his adjutants Mr. Ramsey, Maj. Hatch and Mr. Vanvorhes who were here on their way to make the Indian payment. I found it absolutely necessary to keep strict order and discipline among citizens as well as soldiers and to accomplish this I armed as many citizens as I could and placed them at their posts.*
>
>   TJS Journal

Ft. Ridgely was a fort in name only, and as he rapidly toured its perimeter, Sheehan damned the "lout" who had designed it. It was, in fact, merely a collection of buildings, with huge gaps of space between them, and not even a fence connecting those buildings for cover. With the exception of the barracks, all the structures were of wood. The fort itself was situated on a bluff surrounded on three sides with gullies deep enough to permit a massed enemy to approach to within literally a stone's throw before exposing himself to repelling fire. It seemed designed for ease of assault by any enemy with eyes. And there probably wasn't a Dakota warrior west of Fort Snelling who hadn't walked these same gullies while sauntering in for a social call during the nine years since Ridgely was built. And since this had been Sioux land for generations before the bluecoats came, their familiarity with it had to have been complete.

But whining wasn't going to change matters.

A stone wall roughly a dozen feet on a side and two feet tall had been erected around the parade-ground flagpole. Almost by instinct, Lt. Gere in tow, Sheehan plowed his way through the crowd and mounted the wall, as much to see where his troop had deployed to as to address the hysterical mass of humanity milling about before him. He shouted repeatedly, but failed to draw the crowd's attention, though he could see those in the front rows trying to hush those directly behind them. Finally drawing his service revolver, he fired two rounds into the air and almost immediately drew the silent and wide-eyed attention of any close enough to hear his voice.

Starting with a stern "Now you listen to me!", the senior officer assured his audience that they were now under the protection of over 70 armed troopers, that medical care would be established shortly in the stone building, and that they were to *immediately obey* any order from a blue-uniformed trooper or they would themselves be ejected from the compound.

Telling the crowd that he would return to this spot in 30 minutes to issue further instructions, Sheehan left his stone perch and followed Lt. Gere to Captain Marsh's quarters. There he slammed the heavy plank door and sought an update from the junior officer, all the while chambering two rounds from his cartridge belt should an attack occur within the next several minutes.

The update began with a torrent of fact, opinion and hearsay issued at a rate beyond Sheehan's capacity to absorb. Raising his palm toward the previously untested 19-year-old, Sheehan said "sit", and poured each a full glass from the quarters' water pitcher. For the next ten minutes, the two officers sat, sweated and talked.

Lt. Gere described the scene when the first survivors began rumbling into the fort, wagons overloaded, in some cases the sides burst, horses lathered and spent. At first there was disbelief. Surely those downtrodden curs that begged for table scraps could not have done what was being described. But as more bloodied stragglers began to fill the compound, disbelief turned to grudging and nervous acceptance, and a growing sense of outrage on the part of post commander Marsh. Lt. Gere differed with his commander regarding the extent of the uprising, Gere sensing it was general, Marsh believing that it involved few of the tribe's warriors. But he had always believed his troops to be vastly superior to the Indian fighters, and now eagerly welcomed an opportunity to demonstrate that superiority. Within the hour he had assembled over half his troop strength, issued 40 rounds of ammunition apiece, ordered three freight wagons hitched up, and started his command out toward the ferry crossing to "punish" the savages. But as the newly-arrived survivors saw what appeared to be most of their defenders leaving to what the survivors thought to be certain defeat, their panic grew.

Gere had done his best to deal with the terrified settlers, at first placing the women and children in the barracks building, and ordering any man with arms to stand near one of the outer ring of buildings. This brought out loud and unrelenting resistance from the family members of the men thus put at risk. In all, the smooth-faced Gere had limited success in arming the outer reach of the compound. He did order water brought in from the spring, checked available provisions, directed the ladies to the sanitary facilities, brought out medical supplies from the infirmary, and disbursed his own remaining troops. For the better part of 24 hours he was sole commander of a military cadre of 22 local lads no older than himself, several of whom had been in uniform less than a month.

At about noon of that day, the long-delayed tribal annuity - $71,000 in *gold coin* -was delivered to the fort, which Gere and others spent precious time hiding in a rapidly-dug 5' deep pit adjacent to the flagpole wall.

By 8:00 that night, the ranks of the refugees had swelled to over 100. The first two survivors of the massacre at the ferry had also arrived, telling of the death of Captain Marsh, and the conditions under which the rest were hanging on. Lt. Gere immediately sent another courier – Pvt. Wm. J. Sturgis – out on the quickest mount in the fort to request reinforcements from the commander of Ft. Snelling, and to intercept, if possible, the recruits under Lt. Culver and Agent Galbraith that were even now heading toward that fort.

The dispatch was dated 8:00 PM, August 18:

Capt Marsh left this post at 10 ½ this morning to prevent Indian depredations at the Lower Agency. Some of the men have returned – from them I learn the Capt Marsh is killed and only thirteen of his company remaining. The Indians are killing the settlers and plundering the country. Send reinforcements without delay.

Thomas P. Gere
1st Lieutenant
5th Minnesota volunteers

PLEASE HAND THIS TO GOV. RAMSEY IMMEDIATELY

    Gere did all he could to reassure his growing population of victims, but was himself doubtful of the ability of his tiny cadre to divert even the most minimal assault on the compound. Eight of his remaining troops were sent as outliers, to positions a minimum of 100 yards beyond the garrison's outbuildings. These were issued extra rations of ammunition and water. All were familiar with long guns, and known for their marksmanship. None had previously seen military combat, though three had been with Captain Marsh when he rode to the Agency to defuse the tensions there. All were willing to undertake this sentry duty when ordered, though none had volunteered. They did not need to be cautioned to be alert. Gere spent several minutes, however, reminding the men of the continuing stream of survivors, and for them to make *sure* of their targets before firing their weapons.
    It was almost 9:00 PM before full darkness this August night, and with it went the security of vision.

Hovering clouds made it one of the darkest, as well, a blanket of black punctuated by the moans of the wounded, cries of terrified children, and periodic warning shouts from self-appointed sentries who were sure they saw *something* out there. Fires were extinguished within the compound, and set from the post's dwindling supply of dry firewood along the ridges of the gullies closest to the buildings. These served as weak flares, illuminating any movement that might come from those areas. The remaining troops alternated two-hour lookout shifts with the few civilians who had fled with their arms. Virtually all of the able-bodied men spent the night in the light rain, all structures having been given over to the wounded, women and children. By dawn the chewed-up grounds of Ft. Ripley had been transformed into a quagmire, inches of mud that reduced mobility and added to the general chaos.

  The parade ground was designed to provide space for roughly 90 troopers, in orderly ranks. It was estimated by one of the survivors of the ferry attack that "hundreds" of panicked settlers were by now in the fort. At this point, Ft. Ridgely was already overcrowded to the point of jeopardizing its defense. Where to put the people, the men without arms, the women and children, the elderly? What about food, water? Sanitary facilities? There were over a dozen nervous horses and mules roaming throughout the compound, adding to the bedlam, their owners having leapt from wagons and gone off to find shelter presuming *someone* would care for them. Several families had brought their dogs, now loose and nipping at the heels of the horses. All the survivors were attempting to buttonhole anyone in uniform, thinking them the voice of authority – except the troopers had no answers, and were themselves instinctively edging toward the perimeter to prepare a defense against what all said was imminent attack. Had the raiders attacked then, it was said that blood would have flowed all the way to the river, and this story would never have been told.

CHAPTER TWENTY SEVEN

Sheehan had heard enough of Lt. Gere's nervous prattle. He had said he'd return in 30 minutes, and needed to do so. He had decided to redirect the throng's rampant emotional energy into physical activity. As he broke through the crowd on the way back to his stone "stage" he grew increasingly angry at the invaders, at the obvious inadequacy at the compound that had been supposedly designed to control and defend against them, and at the *need* to be doing all of this. Half a day earlier he and his men had been singing their way to their home fort, anticipating a trip to the southern rebellion they had all signed up to stop in the first place. Now, at best, another diversion; at worst, overwhelming odds and an inability to protect either the settlers or themselves.

This time there was no need for pistol shots to gain the attention of the crowd. As soon as Sheehan mounted the flagpole wall those closest to it began shouting for silence, and within a minute the loudest sounds were of a crying baby, creaking leather tack, and mules slurping at a trough 50 yards away.

"We can protect everyone here", the Lieutenant began, "if you will do exactly what I say, precisely when I say it. We have adequate means of defense, and will need your help to put them in place. Those who choose to ignore my orders, or those of Lt. Gere or the sergeants can leave *now*". No one did.

The fort was located on a table-flat spur of prairie land oriented northwest to southeast, roughly a half-mile north of the Minnesota River. It was isolated on the north and east by deep ravines, running well within musket range to the fort's outlying buildings. About 200 yards to the south the prairie fell off abruptly into the river bed. Only to the west and northwest could an enemy be spotted far enough away to prepare for them; the natural terrain provided ample opportunity to remain hidden until within musket or short-rush range from every other direction. Understanding that a charge from any of those approaches would leave only seconds to prepare, those – military and civilian – who understood the weakness of their position were understandably edgy from their first survey of their defenses.

The garrison pointed toward the northwest. A horseshoe-shaped road came in on the southern edge from New Ulm, fifteen miles to the east, looped toward the northwest on the western side, then took a 90-degree turn back toward the east just north of most of the buildings, enclosing most of those buildings within its broad loop. The parade ground was just within this east-facing horseshoe, as were the stone barracks and officer's quarters, and the flimsier surgeon's office and headquarters building, the commissary, bake-house and laundry. Sgt. Jones' quarters, the stables and tiny hospital were butted up against the road on the north side. The ammunition, stored a distance to prevent catastrophe from accidental discharge, was now some 200 yards from the parade ground, and well within the potential grasp of raiders crawling through the tall prairie grass to the northwest. The warehouse, store, granary, ice and root-houses, and the houses of the suttler and interpreter Quinn, were outside the perimeter of the horseshoe to the west and south. The primary stable was just to the south, at the intersection of the New Ulm Road and one leading directly to the river.

The spring, sole source of drinking water for the fort, was just this side of that distant stable.

Briefly, the Lieutenant laid out a basic plan of defense, including cannon set up virtually within the gullies themselves to preclude attacks from those areas. He set all able-bodied civilians to establishing "walls" of whatever material they could lay their hands on, and digging trenches behind those walls to permit a standing man to remain hidden. He then continued his tour of garrison's perimeter.

"Mother of God", he muttered as he surveyed the setup from the second floor of the stone barracks. "Why not just invite the bastards in for tea?!".

A stockade might have been used to link some of the buildings, but it would have had to exclude the outlying ones, and besides, there was neither time nor material to build one.

The lieutenant noticed a young man looking out from the opposite end of the building, shielding his eyes as he tried to focus on the western horizon. As one of few not racing aimlessly about, he was tabbed by Sheehan to secure the field glasses from Captain Marsh's office, mount the tack shed and watch for signs of the enemy. This lookout would also afford a view of the ravine running toward the fort from the southwest. With that quarter presumably protected from ambush, Sheehan sent a squad of his troopers to set up defensive positions along the closest 100-yard length of the ravine. He arrayed the remainder of his troops along the northern, eastern and southern perimeters of the horseshoe. All the powder and shot he had been returning to Ft. Ripley were hastily distributed to his men, a meager 30 rounds per man. Lt. Gere was tasked with retrieving all of the ammunition in the fort's magazine, identifying any armed – and rational – civilians, and deploying this combined force to supplement the defenses along the entire perimeter.

Sgt. Bishop was ordered to fill in the gaps between the buildings proximate to the parade ground with whatever he could find that might block a bullet or arrow. This second line of defense would provide precious time should the outer barrier be overrun. In the first fifteen minutes, Bishop returned to ask Sheehan if it was OK to use the Captain's desk, and again to see if he might remove a carved door from the barracks building. Swallowing hard to keep himself from losing his own frayed temper on the sergeant, the Lieutenant explained that if they were to lose the upcoming conflict, everything in the fort – themselves included - would go up in flames anyway, and therefore *everything* was available for defensive use – furniture, doors, window frames, straw and hay bales, saddles, wagons, bricks and anything else the sergeant could visualize that might be better than standing out in the open inviting fire.

Surprisingly, a crude defensive perimeter began to be formed. Lt. Gere uncovered a supply of shovels, which were issued to groups of civilians to dig trenches behind their "fortresses" of firewood, old doors, wooden stall lumber and whatever else they could wrench free from its attachment to building or ground. One trooper was assigned to prevent the destruction of the stone wall surrounding the post flagpole.

All of these preparations took place in the span of two hours. Lt. Gere had exhibited creativity and coolness under pressure, and the civilians, once convinced that they were relatively safe under the firepower of the Union troops, also went about their business relatively calmly.

These preparations underway, Sheehan looked to the wounded. Many proved more the victims of shock than life-threatening physical injuries. Those injuries, however, were frequent and gruesome. Many of the women had had their clothing torn, their breasts and arms bruised. Some had portions of their scalp torn out.

Several had been battered and raped. Dozens, more men than women, had open wounds ranging from rifle and shotgun blasts to gaping cleavages in skull, chest, back and extremities. An elderly women had had her right arm hacked off just below the elbow. The woman was alive, but her skin was the color a sheet of paper. She said nothing, and did not cry out, merely looking around without interest. She died within the hour, her body covered with a sheet and laid on a straw bale just behind the barracks building. Many of the survivors suffered burns as they had rushed from cabins set afire by the raiders. Some were serious, flaps of skin falling away from the bared wound, its victim unable to stand the chafing of any cloth covering.

    Victims were first brought to the initial post hospital, a one-room wooded building with plank floor, a sink, counter, a cabinet with a few rudimentary medicines and bandages, and a half-dozen crude bunks. Primitive, but suitable for an outpost where the greatest calamity planned for was an outbreak of poison ivy. It was after this crude clinic filled to overflowing that the barracks building was opened for medical purposes.

    Many of the settlers' wives volunteered as nurses and cooks, and were immediately put to use.

    Benjamin Randall, the post suttler, was charged with producing the greatest possible water supply from the outlying spring, and did so by employing children who were still terrified by what they had experienced. The youngsters performed as hoped, focusing their fears on the task at hand, and utilizing a creative array of vessels to transport the water to the parade ground – glasses, canteens, pails, jugs, flower vases, tubs, wastebaskets, barrels, even a pair of relatively new horse troughs for washing water. Within a matter of hours every available vessel was filled to the brim, and a trench of sorts from the spring to the post was being dug by enthusiastic kids now taken up by their important task.

That process stopped abruptly at 1:00 in the afternoon.

By that time virtually every able soul not otherwise occupied had taken it upon themselves to provide lookout services. Several, under the direction of troopers, stationed themselves at the edges of the ravines that would have provided perfect concealment for an approaching enemy. The bluffs leading down to the river were "manned" by a pair of teenaged girls under the protection of their very formidable German-farmer father and his double-barreled 12-guage shotgun and leather pouch stuffed with shells to feed it.

CHAPTER TWENTY EIGHT

The wriggling on the western horizon came into view almost simultaneously to Sheehan, atop the post's tack shed, and several of the self-appointed lookouts, whose cries of "Indians, Indians!" were accompanied by frantic gestures toward the slow-moving procession yet nearly two miles distant. Through his field glasses Sheehan could see that the column extended beyond the horizon, that it was accompanied by a number of empty buckboards and hay wagons, and that almost all of the warriors were both mounted and armed. The wagons, he supposed, were to be used to carry both booty and female survivors. The natives obviously presumed victory.

Until the point of the sighting, even given the victims and the first-hand reports, most of the troops had harbored an inkling of doubt that they would be personally confronting the savages. It was too unreal. These primitives had always been seen as emaciated, bedraggled, downtrodden. Even if they erupted in a fit of rage, they would soon see the hopelessness of their outburst and flee the inevitable consequences. This the bulk of the troopers truly thought, and so went about their initial preparations – even their forced march back to the fort - dispassionately, even mechanically. But now the bedraggled were before them as warriors, armed, too many to count, with the obvious intent of slaughtering the troopers themselves and all of their charges.

Sheehan dismounted from the roof of the tack shed, then climbed back up for another assessment. By God, there they are, the sons-of-*bitches*, he thought. He had been wrong, largely sympathizing with the plight of the "red men" as he called them. Now, suddenly, every prejudice he had harbored but kept under the surface surfaced. The dirty, stupid, cunning, deceitful *bastards*, he thought. Hatchets in our *backs!* These very individuals he could now see were directly and personally responsible for the gruesome injuries he'd witnessed for the past half day, the gashes and broken and missing limbs and rended flesh of innocent and unarmed settlers, *and* their women and children.

By now most of the troopers had responded to the sentries' outcry, and crowded the mostly-furniture "wall" on the garrison's west side, and a careful observer could see the men's expressions evolve as brows furrowed and jaw muscles twitched. These were no longer "reports". These were the flesh-and-blood instigators of the mayhem described in those reports. Within minutes the nature of the troops' duties changed, from projecting a defensive barrier to administering eye-for-an-eye justice in the most violent imaginable manner. The squirming mass approaching them was no longer an object of fear, but opportunity. The tentative feeling in the pits of the young troopers' stomachs was replaced by a full-blown adrenalin rush that required restraint on the part of at least two of their number, who attempted to climb over the wall and charge the distant horsemen trailing a string of colorful and heartfelt epithets.

While there had been no slacking before, the sighting of the Indian column produced a burst of protective energy that saw remaining doors ripped off their housings, additional wagons overturned, hay bales removed from under horses' noses, and ditches grow deeper by the minute. Women and children were hustled into the non-hospital end of the stone barracks building, and loose horses were simply driven from the compound, with the presumption that they would flee the coming gunfire and be retrievable when it stopped.

Those civilians with arms sought suitable firing positions, while troops set up at the 2nd floor windows of the barracks building, and on its roof. Sgt. John Bishop commandeered a pair of husky young farmers to haul cannon shot to each corner of the compound. And then they waited.

After several minutes, Lt. Gere approached Sheehan's vantage point atop the shed and asked "Are they coming, Lieutenant?".

"Not at this moment", Sheehan responded, without drawing the field glasses from his eyes. "They appear to be having a council".

The council, in fact, turned out to be a power struggle. Little Crow had, without taking the time to consider it, released a monster. Like older leaders anywhere, he favored planning and preparation to secure favorable results in the future. His young men, however, favored action and violence for satisfaction in the present.

The Indian leader was a cunning man. There were many in his party who wanted to take the probably-undefended village of New Ulm, some dozen miles to the east. There there was the possibility of surprise, surely no longer the case at the fort. And there were women, and goods for their wagons. Members of this faction had been encouraging each other during the ride to the fort. Little Crow had said little against the plan during that period. He waited instead to hold council on the matter until directly before the prize he himself sought. Let them see it, he thought. Let them see how easy it will be to take.

In part, he waited until his agitated young warriors were free of the direct influence of Shakopee and Red Middle Voice, the instigators who had forsaken his direction and unleashed their marauders on unarmed civilians. They had operated on emotion, not thought. In that, they were no better than the four young killers who had started this whole series of events. Neither of these men were with Little Crow this afternoon.

Little Crow spoke first in the prairie-side council, describing the riches of the fort in powerful terms – the horses, the food, the powder and lead, the cannon, the helpless survivors, the few defenders. He did not know that Sheehan's troops had already arrived. He felt that the fort was the gate to victory for his people. With the soldiers vanquished, with no protection, every settler in southern Minnesota would hear and flee in terror. Those lands would be theirs again, as would the fine houses built by the intruders. And the road to St. Paul would be open to them.

At this point, the Indian leader was convinced that his forces outnumbered those in the fort by 10 to 1, yet he was unable to persuade his warriors that the fragile compound constituted the easiest pickings. Mazzawamnuna, one of Shakopee's lieutenants, insisted that for every piece of booty available at the fort, the little village of New Ulm held 50 times that amount. And there were *no soldiers* in New Ulm. But there were women. They could have both prizes, fort and village, Mazzawamnuna insisted. Why not take the easiest first? It was simple logic, and it appealed to the bulk of the raiders close enough to hear the argument.

The back-and-forth went on. Those watching from the fort were sure that the discussion involved planning for the coming assault, and used the time to double-check their loads, wriggle deeper into their trenches, and, for most, pray.

Those prayers ultimately seemed to have been heard. Tired of the endless arguing, the respected elder Mankato dismounted and climbed up on the seat of a wagon to address the now milling group. He had brought his band out for the uprising, but he would not torture women or kill children. He would fight, but he had come along to capture the fort. There were enough guns there, he said, to arm all of the warriors, some of whom carried only bows with few arrows, or even hatchets acquired long ago from the traders. And there were cannon to be had too, the big guns. There would be *no* guns to be captured in New Ulm.

Rdainyanka, the fiery son-in-law of the peace chief Wabasha, spoke next. He disagreed with his wife's father, favoring war with the whites. He argued that both prizes could be taken, but only if the Indians acted immediately. He had taken part in the massacre at the Redwood ferry, and knew the white soldiers to be bold fighters, and tenacious when cornered. He called for swift action, before reinforcements could be summoned to either fort or village.

The council continued for fully two more hours, with supporters of a variety of actions each claiming time before the group. Finally the time for a vote came, and over 2/3 of the ballots were for attacking New Ulm.

Little Crow trembled with emotion. Once again, his counsel had been ignored. He condemned Rdainyanka and the others for their lack of thought, of logic, of reality. He had thought the warriors had come to him for *leadership*, when in fact it appeared that their supplications were merely for some form of justification. He had not, in fact, authorized the rampage now underway, the slaughter of civilians, and had even harbored white friends in his own home during the initial bloodletting. Yet it had gone on. He knew by now that it would be called *his* war, but the outrages had gone on in spite of him. And now he had managed to direct the hot-bloods to within sight of what needed to be their primary target, and they *refused to attack it!*

He pointed a shaky finger at the fort and said "Look! See it is as it is now, a prairie hen awaiting your strike. Tomorrow it will be a snarling wolf!".

With that the aging leader roughly reined his horse back toward the west, only to see some 300 of his fighting men and their pack train begin trudging toward the east, and what they thought would be the undefended village of New Ulm.

During the extended council, the fort's occupants had used every minute to shore up their defenses. Cannon were rerouted to better cover the gullies. Several dead trees that had been on the list for removal were downed and dragged by horse team to the compound's perimeter. Additional ammunition was distributed. Nails, broken horseshoes and other shrapnel were gathered to make the cannon even more lethal. A half-dozen cords of firewood were used to plug up holes in the hastily-erected "wall" between the fort's buildings. Many of the trenches were now chest deep. And importantly, the "butterflies" that had marked most of the inexperienced troopers were now settled.

The mood inside the fort became jubilant with the movement of the native force, but only briefly. Was this a ruse? Would the main group continue on until hidden by the trees to the east, then split into smaller war parties to attack the gaps that still remained in the fort's protective shield? Would they come in the night?

Probably not, Sheehan thought. He'd heard that the "old" Sioux disdained fighting at night, a combination of superstition and practicality. Night fighting requires closer quarters; too much potential for harm.

Whatever the Indians' motive, the two lieutenants and both Sgts. Bishop and Kennedy agreed to send out trailing scouts to confirm the movement of the band, and to double the watches in the arroyos and at the bluffs.

No one held the illusion that the potential for attack had passed. Other Indians had accompanied Little Crow as he had headed back toward the agency. Were they to recruit more attackers, to meet up with those returning from New Ulm, possibly as soon as tomorrow?

Except for such questions, the rattling of arms and the makeshift barriers surrounding it, the rhythms of the fort returned at least briefly to something approaching normal. Food was now being prepared, though at half-rations to compensate for the surging population of the garrison. If that population remained more-or-less stable, existing supplies would last some six days, though most expected the siege to be over – one way or another – well before then.

In the hours that followed, the officers and non-coms established a rough command structure that both improved defenses and kept armed settlers occupied. Having had sufficient exposure to those settlers to be able to spot natural leaders, Sheehan appointed several of those who appeared to merit the respect of others as "squad leaders", to gather together those within their ranks to support the troops in the defense of a particular quadrant of the post. Those who were armed were to sweep an assigned sector of the perimeter, backing up individual troopers by firing and reloading alternately with them. Unarmed men were to serve as spotters and ammunition and supply couriers within assigned sectors. Each was to take orders specifically from the trooper assigned to protect that area, who would in turn respond to the normal chain of command. By operating within this structure, the settlers began to see themselves as part of the overall defense mechanism, and remained focused and relatively calm while waiting for the return of the raiders.

The calmness was a reflection of that exhibited by the command structure. Sheehan knew that Lt. Gere had sent couriers to the Governor, to Ft. Snelling, and to Agent Galbraith, who was escorting a couple of dozen half-breed recruits to Ft. Snelling for training. The courier to the Governor had left to the northeast shortly after the first refugees had begun to arrive from the west, and well before the raiders themselves appeared near the fort. So the courier could not have been intercepted by the Indians. Sooner or later, one of those dispatches would have to get through, and reinforcements would begin to arrive.

The other factor contributing to the lack of apparent panic among the fort's command structure had to do with ordnance.

When President Lincoln called for 78,000 troops, Governor Ramsey had been in Washington, and pledged the president the first of those troops, for which he raided the frontier forts including Ridgely. In most instances, raw recruits replaced the experienced soldiers that were taken. Providentially, one of the few professional soldiers left behind was Ordnance Sgt. John Jones, master of the six pieces of artillery left at Ft. Ridgely. For several months prior to the incidents at the Lower Agency, the recruits were drilled daily, in part to retain military discipline, in part to shore up military skills. During this period, Sgt. Jones, a passionate advocate for his "big guns" as well as a highly-skilled practitioner, drilled members of Company B "unmercifully" on the operation and tactics of cannon-fire warfare. At first there was resistance. What Jones had the men doing was hard, grimy work, wheeling the several-hundred-pound units around like overgrown handguns. Gradually, as their teamwork and their performance improved, the complaints died down. Ultimately, the man began calling themselves "cannoneers", with more than a hint of pride.

Sgt. Jones spent much of this day in touring the post's defenses, offering suggestions, re-placing his beloved guns to achieve maximum efficiency, and coordinating the placement of pyramids of cannon shot.

While these preparations were underway, courier Sturgis, using several horses, covered the 125 miles to Ft. Snelling in under 18 hours. On the way, he found Agent Galbraith's Renville Rangers camped near Glencoe, just 42 miles east of Ft. Ridgely. While the Sioux raiders were hurrying down the New Ulm Road to wreak havoc on the town, the rangers returned on the nearly parallel road from St. Peter, several miles to the north. These, too, were new recruits, willing to risk death to fight on the side of the Bluecoats against the south. It was their selection that had caused some of the renegades to think that the Union had reached the bottom of the barrel in selecting their warriors, and thus might be vulnerable to attack. As it turned out, this group had somehow been able to acquire 50 old Harper's Ferry muskets in St. Peter, and enough powder and shot for *three rounds apiece* – with which they willingly returned to face hundreds of full-bloods who had already demonstrated their capacity for savagery.

Marching full out, the 24-member Ranger contingent made it back to the fort within hours of the departure of the Sioux raiders. Their arrival was once again celebrated with joy approaching hysteria, prolonged cheers, gunshots, even a single cannon shot.

Lt. Sheehan shared in those moments of celebration, though now faced with the need to efficiently array a force that had reached 180 effectives, protecting nearly 300 refugees. Little Crow's prediction that the fort would become a "snarling wolf" was becoming true.

CHAPTER TWENTY NINE

New Ulm was a young town, but thriving, and the closest of any size to the Indian agencies. It had been founded by members of German colonization societies some six years earlier, and had a population of nearly 900 at the time of the outbreak. Not only did it present the prospect of more booty than available at the fort, but the town itself gave the advantage clearly to any attacker in the event of a siege. Its sturdy homes were spread out on a pair of broad terraces rising from the Minnesota River to a bluff some 200 feet above. By approaching the city from the bluff, conveniently covered with thick woods, an attacking force could claim the advantages of both surprise and gravity, firing down on the occupants with either rifle or bow.

Ironically, the townsfolk had gathered on August 18 to provide a festive send-off to a party of recruiters heading west to sign up members of the booming farming communities to join the war effort in the south. It was this party, returning in terror after having been ambushed as they passed through nearby Milford Township, that provided the early warning necessary to have prevented what surely would have been a slaughter greater than that at Redwood Ferry.

Two men, Sheriff Charles Roos and military veteran Jaccob Nix, probably prevented outright panic by organizing the men who had guns into militia units. Unfortunately, the town could muster only 44 guns. These were concentrated into a downtown area of approximately three blocks square, surrounded largely by sturdy single- and two-story brick buildings, affording both protection and wide angles of fire from window and rooftop. Couriers were sent out to St. Peter and other settlements both for assistance and to issue warnings. Sheriff Roos led parties through the surrounding area, alerting farmers to their plight, and bringing in those who understood the danger. For some reason, no attack was mounted that day, perhaps because, once again, the Sioux would have been required to fight at in the night.

The Sioux might have rested; the defenders did not. By 4:00 AM a New Ulm courier was banging on the door of one of the founders of the town of St. Peter, William Dodd, who immediately launched a protective-force recruiting drive in his community. The courier then rode to Travers des Sioux to awaken Charles Flandrau, a respected Minnesota Supreme Court justice, member of the state's constitutional convention, and one of its best-known citizens. Judge Flandrau woke immediately and rode to St. Peter, where he found Dodd, who had already gathered nearly a hundred volunteers. While they were rounding up arms and supplies, sixteen more mounted men showed up at New Ulm around 1:00 AM on the 19th.

Little Crow's force, without a leader at the moment, had fatally underestimated the defenders at New Ulm. They were mostly German immigrants, a hardy, hard-working and bull-headed set, many of whom spoke no English. There was little fear among them; most of their exposure to the red man had come in the form of beggars at their door, none of whom, individually, were imposing enough to frighten. And the Germans were as territorial about their small plots as the Sioux were their larger one. They weren't about to be put off as they marshaled their small force, including fighters with 14 rifles, 12 shotguns, and 18 double-barreled shotguns. Another dozen or so with weapons chose to stay to protect their families or place of business rather than join the defense force downtown.

That area had been converted in short order to a respectable version of a fortress. Overturned wagons, barrels, bales and other material quickly filled the narrow spaces between the 2-story brick buildings, and men were effectively placed at those barriers, and on the floors and roofs of the buildings. Even the "unarmed" presented a formidable force, equipped as a reserve unit with revolvers, axes, and any other implement of defense that was at hand.

It wasn't until 3:00 that afternoon that the First Battle of New Ulm started, but instead of the 300 who had left Little Crow, there were little more than 100. Some had drifted off in unknown directions. At least half had left the New Ulm party after a bitter dispute, and headed south, where they continued to prey on unprotected civilians and set fields ablaze wherever they were dry enough to catch.

The 100 surrounding New Ulm acted more like a drunken youth gang than fearsome warriors. They appeared to follow the loudest yeller. Initially they circled the town just beyond gun range, then, without any apparent communication, all charged the southern barricades. It was as if they were being discharged through a giant funnel, a gruesome variation of follow-the-leader. When they were driven back by intense fire, they all ran to the northwest, held a hasty conference, and all charged from that quarter. Again, no success. Finally they returned to their original outlying circle, more or less, and charged with no coordination whatever, from wherever they stood. Here and there a raider would succeed in leaping the barrier, only to be beaten or shot. A few made it back out.

The defenders fell, as well. Five died in these initial assaults, all among those manning the ground barriers. Those in or on the buildings succeeded in pouring frightening, if not always accurate, fire down at the Indians, with only one of their number being hit – an arrow through the bicep. A particularly tragic death was that of Emilie Pauli, a brave 13-year-old girl who ran across a street to rescue her cat and was cut down by what must have been a random shot. While agonizing, her death had the result of enraging the defenders as a group, even further committing them to a to-the-death defense of their city. Another half-dozen defenders were wounded in the episode, mostly superficial but for 17-year-old Eric Goettl, shot in the stomach, who died a slow and unpleasant death.

The common impression left from the first attack was how disorganized it was. Little Crow had turned back by the fort. There was no leader, and no plan. It seemed that the force that did attack the village got discouraged by the effectiveness of the return fire and didn't know how to circumvent it. Then, around 6:00 that evening, the skies opened up and poured a prodigious amount of water onto the bluff and the town, accompanied by high winds and thunder claps sufficient to frighten the horses and cause participants on both sides to plug their ears. Again, the opportunity to sneak past the defenders in the dark was ignored, with the invaders slipping away back past the fort, their ardor for blood at least temporarily cooled.

Shortly after their departure, the ranks of the city's defenders grew by some 125 Frontier Guards under Judge Flandreau, and three physicians to serve as needed.

CHAPTER THIRTY

Taoyateduta returned at a trot all eleven miles from the fort to the agency, though there really was no hurry. He must have thought he still had much "medicine", given that he passed a number of refugees still streaming toward the fort, and none were armed. But his thoughts focused on more than personal harm. Already, he knew, the whites were saying "Little Crow's gone on the warpath", "Little Crow's killing women and children". One settler, just before being shot in the leader's presence, had said there would be a bounty on his head "...big enough to bring the buffalo hunters in from the territories." This had *not* been his war. It had been thrust upon him. He was not a slaughterer. There were those who claimed he had never fired a shot in battle. He was Taoyateduta, an orator, a respected elder. He had been denied the speakership of his tribe; was he now to be condemned as a bloodthirsty renegade, he who had once sat in the office of the Great Father himself, the President of the United States?

Disillusioned and caught up with his own thoughts, he made his way back to his brick home after midnight. He sat inside on the dirt floor where his words had triggered the events he now rejected, dozing fitfully, until wakened by a racket nearly as compelling as the one he'd responded to two days earlier. Was it only two days? Was this then?

Outside, plodding through a sea of mud caused by hours of misty rainfall, stood the same leaders he had attempted to counsel both here and before the fort, "leaders" who had gone on to New Ulm and were now standing once more before his lodge – for *what?*

For a moment, bleary-eyed from lack of sleep and hours of bitter contemplation, the elder simply looked from his door, not comprehending what was before him. Twice now these people who would not return his glare had insulted him by ignoring his counsel. Where once there was a chance, slight but *possible*, for victory, each step they had taken on their own had brought them further from it. He had agreed to give his *life* for a cause sparked by four hot-headed *children*. They owed him loyalty, and had withheld it. He owed them nothing!

He turned, as if to abandon them as they had him, but instead whirled and spat "Where is your booty? Where are your new wives? Where is the blood on your hands from grappling with the enemy? *Tell me!*"

Like simple children being chastised for being naughty, the beleaguered warriors cast their eyes aside and looked at one another, waiting for one of their number to respond. Finally, Mazzumnama spoke, excusing their reluctance to attack at night, glorifying their hail of bullets from the bluffs, boasting about the number of killed and wounded with a loss of but two of their own. Before he could continue, Little Crow shot out one hand and shouted "Stop!". "You left a gift at the fort for an 'easier' prize. Where is your prize? Where is your booty. Where are your women? Did you go to sit on a hill and shoot anything that squirmed below? *Why did you go there?*"

It wasn't a question he expected to be answered. The omens to this point were all bad; uncontrolled killing; failure to follow orders, or listen to reason; inability to defeat lightly-armed civilians! The tide of battle appeared to be shifting before the battle had begun. And the life of this battle, he was becoming certain, would end with his own.

He knew now that the possibility of ultimate victory had passed. He knew of the force that would soon be arrayed against them, and the futility of resistance even now. At best, there might come an opportunity for negotiation, but if the indiscriminate slaughter of civilians continued, he knew there would *be* no negotiations; the whites would wipe all who did not flee from the map with as little mercy as they themselves had been shown.

"Why are you *here*?" he rasped at the faces nearest him. For what seemed like minutes, there was only muttered response. Finally the old warrior drew himself up and scolded "I will tell you why. Because you broke out like a pack of hungry wolves without a leader. You hunted by instinct, without seeing. But does even the wolf hunt for revenge? It hunts to *survive*. Your survival was to be found in the blood of the bluecoats, but you sought revenge on the unarmed, and trinkets, and to lose yourselves in the loins of white women. And what did you bring back? *Bodies!* Whose bodies are they, whose sons and brothers? And how many more will there be when the snarling wolf is finally attacked, now with five *times* the arms inside. It is as I said. *What would you have me do now?*".

Little Crow paused, shaking his head grimly. In a moment, having accepted his own death and made up his mind, he went slowly to one knee, and beckoned down the stair to Mazzumnuma. Speaking in a low growl, he told the old man to address his warriors and determine if they were willing to commit to his leadership, to follow him without question in the days ahead. If not, he said, take them and flee, because certainly the gallows awaited them for their mindless slaughter of women and children. If they agreed to follow him, the elder was to return to Little Crow when the day was full with every fighter mounted and armed. Either way, he would now sleep. If they refused, he had released a monster, and could do nothing more. It they agreed, tomorrow would be a day for him longer than any other.

CHAPTER THIRTY ONE

The warriors argued until interrupted by morning birdsong, then – seeing no alternative and realizing that no one else could unite the tribal factions – agreed to be led by Little Crow. That was the reason they chose him in the first place. His rage was understandable, but he couldn't just walk away now; it *was* his war. The braves sent out runners to all factions to meet at the agency by mid day, and most responded.

Some said Taoyateduta was a visionary; others dismissed him as a dreamer. If nothing else, he was a planner. In the hectic 48 hours since the breakout began, he had argued for caution, laid out an order of battle, verbally sparred with his recalcitrant warriors, protected his friends – and produced the grand plan for victory over what all Sioux saw as the weakened troops in southern Minnesota.

The plan called for the Winnebagoes to ply the Minnesota River from Mankato to St. Paul, the Chippewa to come down the Mississippi from Crow Wing to St. Paul, and the lower Sioux to take the land route between the two rivers through the big woods, meet the others at their confluence, and make a mass charge at Ft. Snelling itself.

But the plan remained a theory. Neither the Winnebago nor the traditional enemies the Chippewa granted it much enthusiasm, and the still-raving lower Sioux could not focus on any activity that did not bear fruit by the end of the day. It was all Little Crow could do to coordinate the actions of the growing mass of local warriors, most of whom joined because of the zeal of their "leaders", and the ease with which the dreaded whites had fallen under the initial assault. Some Winnebagos did show up late in the day, as did a small band of upper Sioux anxious to establish their reputations as warriors, but the turnout was meager as compared to the mighty Sioux nation.

    By early afternoon Little Crow had mustered nearly 800 warriors, each carrying his own memories of humiliation, or starvation, or physical abuse at the hands of the intruders, and each stoking the fires of hatred in all within hearing. It was a milling, jostling mob of fighters, barely under control, most astride gaunt ponies, wondering why and how Little Crow had resumed the role of leader. Though a crude array of humanity, it was formidable in armament, number and purpose. This time, Taoyateduta led from the front.

CHAPTER THIRTY TWO

    A malaise of sorts had set in at the fort, particularly among the settlers who were not part of the post's defense. There had been a sense of urgency for such an extended period that now that all had been done that *could* be done with the materials at hand, most of the nearly 500 occupants simply succumbed to physical and emotional exhaustion, and sat or laid on any available patch of open ground. A single overturned wagon and a sheet of ripped canvas barricaded an open-air outhouse hastily dug near the northeast corner of the compound, with the line before – men, women and children – seldom dropping below a dozen. In all, there was an eery quiet for such a large gathering. Remarkably, few slept. Fewer still spoke.

    Pickets had been set out at every vantage point, yet it was now approaching the end of the second day since the slaughter began, and no raiders had been sighted since they had passed on toward New Ulm. Lt. Sheehan walked the perimeter of the post on several occasions, advising troopers to double-check both weapons and ammunition supply, and to keep a weather-eye out for movements in the prairie grass that surrounded them. Sgt. Jones' men had become the de-facto sentries over the arroyos and gullies practically butting up against the post due to the placement of their cannon, and the Sergeant kept up a never-ending stream of suggestions and encouragement to make certain they were prepared for the assault the experienced non-com was sure would come.

    More water was brought in. Horses and mules were tied up outside the buildings to make room for people – and to provide decoys for any warrior aching to expand his wealth by a couple of chubby white-man's ponies. It was eerie; so quiet.

It was slightly before 1:00 PM on the afternoon of August 20 that the quiet time proved to be over. Most of the occupants had been assigned specific locations if and when an attack seemed imminent, some designed simply to keep them out of the way. It took only two words to get them into those locations – "Riders coming!".

The phrase, repeated even louder -"Riders coming! *Lots* of riders!" - came from Kaleb Traficante, a responsible 16-year old who had eagerly commandeered the post telescope upon his arrival, and had perched himself atop the suttler's house some 200 yards west of the parade grounds. Having made his announcement, and realizing the precarious nature of his position so far from the protection of the compound, the young man swung down from the rooftop and scooted back to gasp his finding to Lt. Sheehan. From atop the tack shed Sheehan was able to confirm the report, and that the approaching column consisted of no less than several hundred Sioux. His stomach tightening, Sheehan ordered the bugler to blow Assembly, and ordered troopers to their posts, and all settlers inside. It was beginning.

The men, for the most part, went about their tasks quietly, their expressions grim. Some of the women let out what many of the men must have been feeling. Many crossed themselves, others went to their knees where they stood. One relatively young woman, whose 7-year-old daughter had been brutally killed before her eyes, commenced to scream unintelligible curses. She was led away gently by other women, and could be heard sobbing in Captain Marsh's office during the entire engagement.

The silence on the barriers was broken more than once by the sounds of wretching.

The column approached the fort deliberately, then halted. A rider on a white horse – everyone remembered the color of the horse – approached to just beyond rifle range to the west of the fort. One of the defenders of the western barrier fired. Sheehan, having yet to issue orders to fire, hollered at the man to stop. Through his 'scope, he could confirm the figure atop the horse to be Little Crow, who sat calmly as the trooper's spent ball landed a good 20 yards before him. The Sioux leader was yelling something toward the fort, but was too distant to be heard. From his southwest gun position, Sgt. Jones picked up a few words, and swore softly. The warriors who had trooped by two days ago were leaderless. The defenders were not to be so lucky today.

Out of range, Little Crow kept up something of a show for nearly a half-hour, yelling, waving a handful of warriors to his side, sending them fanning north and south, then back to the column.

Sgt. Jones clambered up to Sheehan's observation point, and suggested that he interrupt this diversion with a six-pound cannon ball. Sheehan agreed with the idea, but resisted the diversion that would have created within his own ranks, and instead ordered the sergeant to strengthen the watch on the gullies.

Indians appeared on west side of garrison about 1 oclk p.m. and commenced fighting about 2 oclk surrounded the garrison on all sides and commenced attack a number of them crawling into the outbuildings and ravines that surround the garrison which afforded them great shelter and got close enough to the garrison building to set fire raise the windows and fired several shots at Ordnance Sergeant Jones – Lady who was rescued from her fearful position by a squad of Co c resulting at the time in killing Mark M Grear a private of Co C who was shot in mouth and killed instantly had a little Satisfaction by seeing 3 of the Indians shot dead at the same time put out fire that had been set by the Indians the soldiers occupying the buildings and in such daring attempts we fought the red devils fearless (sic) and boldly until dark at which time they fell back and camped about 1 mile from the garrison where I could hear them distinctly council all night the night previous 4 half breeds deserted from company named Renville Rangers stuffing our cannon with rags before they left this caused great confusion with the gunners who had to draw the cartridges and found their guns stuffed with rags this convinced (sic) me that there was no trust to be put in half breeds I immediately arrested 2 other half breeds who had said they would desert the next night and thus ended the day resulting as follows Number of killed and wounded Mark M Grear of Co C killed instantly Robert Baker of renville rangers killed instantly 2 citizens killed, wounded Harris Porter Shortridge of Co C.

TJS Journal
Wednesday, Aug 20, 1862

CHAPTER THIRTY THREE

Sgt. Jones had barely turned from his exchange with Lt. Sheehan when Little Crow and about 20 of his warriors charged the western perimeter of the garrison with shrieks and weapons firing, only to be met with withering fire from the nearly 40 defenders of that barrier. Three of the attackers fell from their horses, and two of the animals were hit, one spilling its rider, the other careening away from the line, screaming from the shock of the .50 caliber ball. The loose rider, obviously injured, was picked up as the braves retreated from the fort's robust response.

The attack by the cunning leader had served as a signal for a simultaneous charge from the fort's eastern flank. Marked by a cacophony of curses from inside the fort, painted heads and bare chests streamed out of the ravine that reached within 50 yards of the compound. They, too, were met with concentrated rifle and pistol fire, interspersed by the blasts from the Indians' double-barreled shotguns and the *boom-booms* of Sgt. Jones strategically-place 6- and 12-pound howitzers. Though all involved later swore that a hundred or more of the savages had burst out of the ravine, all except two miraculously disappeared back into the ground in response to the lead balls whistling all around them and churning up the dirt at their feet. The two charges had left the defenders momentarily confused, but they rapidly recovered and spent the next several minutes congratulating each other on their "victories".

The officers and non-coms split up during this respite to bring the celebrants back to reality, and make certain that their attention remained focused on their assigned sector. They had won no battle, but they had won time, that gratefully used to reload weapons and check for damage. Amazingly, only two defenders suffered wounds, they, having stood side by side, inflicted with minor buckshot punctures from the same shell.

Up until those attacks, there had been a handful of settlers in favor of "negotiating" with the Indians, who felt that if they weren't made angry, they would spare the settlers' lives, that the poor devils, after all, were just after goods, and would most likely be on their way. These pacifists abandoned that position following the attacks, and could be seen seeking shelter under furniture in and around the stone barracks building.

Initially, Sheehan placed himself on the earthen platform surrounding the parade ground flagpole, affording himself an overall view at least of the defenses between the buildings, and the ground beyond those openings. He was thus able to direct efforts based on enemy movements, though he was obliged to commandeer two privates to carry messages after having to outshout the combatants' explosives during the first assault.

Given the volume of rounds exchanged on both sides, Sheehan and his staff expressed amazement that more bodies didn't litter the battlefield, after even this initial attack.

The assault had started along the western edge of the compound, but gradually appeared to concentrate in the northeast quadrant. Some of the outbuildings north of the barracks were taken over by the Sioux, including the log cabins across the northern road. A number of the buildings were set on fire, including the home of Sgt. Jones.

"Be damned if they will." was the only utterance by the taciturn veteran, but those within hearing saw a new set to the man's jaw as he re-set another of his six-pounders at the outlet of the eastern ravine, and armed himself with a 12-guage.

The northern view from the compound was well-covered, with fourteen windows on the second floor of the barracks building looking out, and three men at each window – two loading, one firing. One, Private McFall, reported that return fire hit the building "like hail in a storm". A civilian, Ezmon Earle, also fought from the barracks. He ducked, he said, more from the war whoops than from live ammunition. In all, these 42 men repulsed charge after charge on the northern sector, with the loss of but a single man, Private Mark Greer, of Company C, who received a fatal head wound while manning one of the corner windows.

Two artillery crews defended the northern sector of the post as well. Sgt. James McGrew of Company B commanded the first gun. The second was directed by a civilian, J. C. Whipple, who had served in the army during the Mexican war. He was older, and not as agile as the younger McGrew, but at the completion of events he was given a nod as the equal of any cannoneer west of the Mississippi. Whipple's gun was positioned between the bakery and laundry buildings on the northeast corner of the post, McGrew's on the northwest. Both were able to move sufficiently outside the line of the buildings to be able to fire along either axis, north/south or east/west. At the point of most concentrated attack from the east, McGrew's gun covered the northern edge of the east sector, while Whipple was able to rake the territory directly before him to the east, north and all the way south. This he did with sufficient accuracy to keep the marauders' heads down. They feared the big guns, and with good reason.

The cannon fired both heavy lead balls and spherical case shot, tubes containing bullets, shrapnel, and their own fused explosive. The big gun essentially lofted these shells over the enemy. If the fuse had been set at the proper length, they would explode over or among them, wreaking bloody havoc over a wide area. They were called "devil guns" by the Indians, who had no defense against them.

In the case of the initial charge, a particularly hot fire was coming from the stables to the northeast of the post, and from the depressed area directly surrounding them. Troopers shooting from the north-facing barracks couldn't stick their heads out the windows long enough to aim toward the stables without exposing themselves to fire from raiders directly in front of them, shooting from the log houses across the road. Similarly, defenders from Company C were occupied keeping the attackers from swarming over the parade ground from the eastern ravine, and could afford neither the time nor the exposure necessary to assist the defenders at the northeast corner.

The problem was solved in an instant when Sgt. McGrew, after an ill-timed shot that exploded well beyond the target, set his fuse accurately and exploded a shrapnel-shell directly in the center of the entrenched raiders, sending bodies and parts of bodies flying, and those still living fleeing.

After an exchange of fire for what seemed like hours but was in fact less than one, and an apparent withdrawal of enemy forces from the east, roughly half the men from Company C advanced to retake the still-standing buildings north of the barracks, and saw the Sioux melt away from there as well, back to the arroyo on the east through which they'd come.

It was a brief respite.

Within ten minutes - and without celebrations – the post was attacked by another roughly 200 warriors who charged the fort from below the river bluffs and through the ravine approaching from the south and southwest. Little Crow could be seen on his white horse, parading back and forth like some European general, encouraging his braves, whacking their horses with a staff he carried.

"Gere!" Sheehan shouted. "Come here!"

The younger lieutenant leapt up on the earthen platform, instinctively ducking, immediately aware of the exposure it imposed.

"They're attacking *sequentially!*" The younger officer looked puzzled.

"They're testing our defenses in sequence. There must be 400 of the red bastards. If they hit us on all sides at once, we'll be in a shitpot 'o trouble, but they *aren't!* It looks like they didn't like what they saw on the east side, so now they're trying' us on the south and west. Focus as many riflemen over there as room allows, but keep the east covered in case it's a feint. I don't think it is, but we don't know how tricky this guy is yet. If I'm right, he'll jump to the northwest next. We've got ample ammo, but tell the shooters to *pick their targets*. We're not going to win this with noise alone."

Lt. Gere, nodding, said simply "Done.", and hurried off to deliver Sheehan's orders. Two squads from Company C were left to patrol the fort's eastern edge, those troops having pulled in to the buildings on that side of the parade ground. The remainder were sent to jostle for position at the already crowded southwest and western barriers. Some of the Indians, probably fewer than a dozen, had been left behind on the east side as harassers, and would occasionally pop up and fire either rifle or bow. Somehow the notion of being struck through by an arrow spooked the defenders more than being shot by rifle or shotgun. While growing in confidence, none were cocky, and all remained alert and concealed as much as possible.

Within an hour, the eastern attackers had slithered back down their gully, apparently called back to reinforce the west-side assault.

Little Crow had apparently expressed dismay at his warriors' inability to breach the eastern defenses, and called for the attack on the southwest quadrant in an attempt to scatter the fort's defenses. To a certain extent he was successful. The fire from the southwest and west was sufficiently hot for Sheehan to order Sgt Jones to supplement the rifle fire with his 6-pounder, particularly in the opening between the officer's quarters and and the post HQ. This was the most open area available to the raiders, with better than 60 yards between the two buildings, and no other structures nearby save the primary stables across the road over 100 yards to the south. Attempts had been made to fill the gap with earthen mounds, downed trees, and three overturned wagons, but it was an inviting space for the invaders, and they focused their fire upon it.

The firing, in fact, had soon become general. While there was a pause in the Indians' attempts to enter the post proper, there was none in their attempts to take potshots at any movement within the fort.

Where in hell did they get all this ammunition, Sheehan thought. They must have had stores of it buried for years. Were we so certain we had them whipped we simply failed to keep our eyes open? We would pay for that.

At about this time Sgt. Jones approached Sheehan and acknowledged that the raiders appeared able to sustain the assault for some time, and that all of the ammunition for the cannon that was inside the perimeter of the fort might be used up.

Was there no more?, Sheehan inquired. Yes, said Jones, while directing his gaze away from his commander. It seemed that Sheehan's earlier orders to bring all powder and shot in from the ammo magazines outside the fort had not, in the initial confusion, been carried out. The two privates charged with the task would be disciplined, Jones said, but...

That discipline might include losing their hair, Sheehan replied, red-faced. What *now*, Sergeant? he asked.

Jones said he felt confident of his ability to retrieve the critical supplies. The magazine, he pointed out, stood on the prairie to the northwest, the only direction that did not provide the enemy with a ravine to hide in or trees to lurk behind. He would set up a field of fire, and use a wagon with a driver and two loaders to rush to the magazine and retrieve its contents. He pointed out that the magazine stood within the direct line of sight of the 14 men shooting from the north side of the barracks building.

Without a reasonable alternative, Sheehan approved the risky maneuver, with the caveat that Jones himself was not to go. Losing ammunition would be bad; losing the artillery master would be calamitous.

Within 20 minutes the barracks shooters had been notified, a driver and two loaders recruited, and a mule and wagon brought to the northwest barrier. At a signal, 20 feet of the barrier were hastily torn down, and the already nervous mule lashed out that gate toward the magazine. Simultaneously, a perimeter of fire was laid down to the west and southwest, and a single barrage from Mr. Whipple's 12-pound howitzer added for effect. The barrage of fire performed as hoped, with Indians already drifting toward the northwest corner driven back while the loaders completed their work. Within ten minutes from start to finish, the ammunition magazine was emptied and its contents safely delivered back to the fort. After agreeing with the three participants that it was the longest ten minutes of their lives, Sheehan congratulated the men and indicated that their efforts were heroic, and worthy of a commendation. He would see to it.

Sgt Jones took immediate command of the ammunition, storing some in the lower level of the barracks building and distributing the rest to his six crews of cannoneers.

For the next five hours, the besieged defenders went through what Sheehan later described as the "...*firy (sic) gates of hell.*". The Indians lacked the firepower of the whites, but made up for it through their fearlessness and tactics of intimidation. From their garishly-painted bodies to their shrieks and guttural threats to the hit-and-run methods of attack, they kept up an incessant pressure that the defenders realized could only result in death should they let their guard down for an instant. Some civilians could be seen leaving their positions and stumbling toward the center of the parade ground, just shaking their heads and *admitting* defeat.

But there were the heroes, too. The barriers that had been erected seldom reached the height of a man – most were waist high - and the Indians would send bursts of fire over them like swarms of angry hornets, so much lead that it could be actually seen whizzing through the air. Yet the couriers and ammo suppliers ran through this barrage with barely a hesitation. When one of the defenders would be wounded, Mrs. Muller would come right out from the hospital and supervise initial care and transport to the stone barracks. By the end of the day she would have so much blood on her arms and clothing that at first glance it seemed certain she would have to collapse from loss of blood. And never so much as a word of complaint.

Lt. Gere wheeled the men of Company C around as if they were a single multi-legged creature, providing covering fire for the cannon crews, filling in gaps wherever they occurred, and challenging any rush to overcome the post's perimeter. Gere himself carried the look of excitement, not fear, as if he were manning the goalposts of some game or other. He proved an uncommonly courageous man, a characteristic that was later to earn him the Medal of Honor.

For those who overcame the normal nervousness of battle, much of the earlier hesitation had congealed into a healthy rage at what the red devils had done. In one instance, as dusk fell, a pair of attackers made the stables north of the compound. With the accuracy of a rifleman, cannoneer Whipple sent two shells into the building, setting the hay inside on fire. As one of the Indians on the inside fled, he was shot in the legs and fell, whereupon two mixed-bloods who had stayed to defend the fort – Joe Latour and George Dashner – ran toward the helpless fellow, picked him up and threw him bodily back into the flames. His screams could be heard above the din, and were the object of raucous cheers from all who witnessed.

CHAPTER THIRTY FOUR

As darkness fell, so did real rain. During the day the garrison had been under a sort of thick mist that would lift occasionally to allow defenders to observe enemy movements, just enough moisture to make everything damp, accumulate in the soil, and keep everyone both dirty and uncomfortable. Enough, too, to keep powder damp if it wasn't kept under shirts and saddle blankets, in canisters, or in at least one case the foot part of a trooper's upended boot. Surely the Indians' powder was subject to the rain as well, the Lieutenant thought, noting with relief the drop-off in volume of firing from outside the compound. Soon enough spotters alerted Sheehan to the movement of the attackers away from the fort.

Placing pickets on all four corners, Sheehan met with Lt. Gere, Sergeants Jones and McGrew, and Dr. and Mrs. Muller to review what damage had been done at the fort, and what impact the vigorous defense may have had on Little Crow's warriors.

The good news was that, in spite of the size and tenacity of the onslaught, and the hundreds of balls that had struck the fort's barriers, only one defender had been killed, and four wounded. None of the wounds was life-threatening. The perimeter had held; there were no irreparable breaches. Only two fires had broken out from the volley of fire-arrows aimed at the buildings' damp walls and roofs, and those were readily extinguished. The half-breed deserters' attempts to sabotage the cannon had been discovered before true damage might have been done. Most importantly, all agreed, was that previously "green" troops and civilians had come through what was probably the best the Indians could throw at them, had fought courageously, and had *won*. Instead of apprehensive amateurs, Fort Ridgely was now defended by 180 battle-hardened veterans. It took some hours, but as that realization grew, the growth in individual confidence could be physically seen. The troops had prevailed when they didn't know what was coming. Now they *did* know what would be coming, what their weakness were the first time around, and how to fix them. Sheehan, Gere and the two sergeants walked the perimeter for the next two hours, gathering intelligence, distributing ammunition, ordering repairs, and commanding all defenders to sleep in alternating 4-hour shifts beginning immediately. It was approximately 10:00 PM when they completed their rounds. It was doubtful that many in that first sleeping shift got their full four hours.

  The night itself was eerily quiet, particularly so in contrast to the incessant roar of the previous day. The rain had subsided; there was no breeze. There were crickets, helpful in that they tended toward silence when confronted with potential danger – such as a human in their midst. And there were mosquitoes, who returned with ferocity once the noise and acrid smoke had cleared the compound. It was hovering near 90 degrees during most of the evening, cooling off just a bit before daybreak. The sounds around the perimeter were mostly slaps, and the flapping of shirts to create hints of a breeze. Conversations among those still awake were carried on in hushed tones. It was anything but a comfortable night, but given the respite from violence it was gratefully received.

  The break of day following proved mundane. There were nearly 500 people needing to be fed, watered, clothed, provided sanitary facilities. Supplies were low. Pup tents with pails had been set up as additional privies. A wagon with a half-dozen barrels was sent under heavy guard to retrieve water from the spring. At half-rations, sufficient food was inventoried to last for four days. Snacks of salt-crackers and jerky were distributed, with the "real" food to be prepared during the night and supplied the following morning.

    The barriers were next to gain attention. With most of the transportation animals missing, now-surplus bags of oats were added to the "walls" between buildings, more to disguise a shooter's location than stop a bullet or arrow. The compound and the area immediately outside were scoured for rocks and branches, as were the first 50 feet or so of the arroyos that were so successful in hiding attackers the previous day. Trenches were dug even deeper. A couple of smoldering stall walls from the stables were brought up and propped outside stretches that were mostly made up of branches.

    It was just after 7:00 AM that the first shots of the day rang out. Coming from the southeast gully, they appeared to be covering fire for the Indians to recover bodies. Though it was not known for certain, it was believed that at least six Sioux had died during the previous day's action. Though the firing lasted only for about an hour, it had the effect of keeping the defenders on edge throughout the day. At 4:00 PM it resumed spasmodically, though with greater effectiveness; three of the defenders were slightly wounded.

    Sheehan and Gere conferred regarding the potential for reinforcements, confirming that Gere had sent an urgent dispatch to Governor Ramsey. Sheehan's troops had covered 42 miles in under 10 hours. Surely by now the courier had reached St. Paul and relief would be on its way. The post's position was anything but favorable. Food, ammunition and medical supplies were all low. There were now six wounded whose need for medical help increased as the hours went by. Children were becoming understandably irritable; some were still in a state of shock. It wasn't known if Little Crow had gone back for reinforcements, or was even now sending attackers stealthfully up the arroyos on three sides of the fort. The feeling within the fort was one not only of peril, but isolation.

Sheehan decided to send another urgent dispatch to the governor, with only a touch of Celtic embellishment.

Ft. Ridgely, Aug 21st 2PM
Gov. Alexander Ramsey
We can hold this place but little longer unless reinforced. We are being attacked almost every hour, and unless assistance is rendered we cannot hold out much longer. Our little band is becoming exhausted and decimated. We had hoped to be reinforced today, but as yet can hear of none coming.
T. J. Sheehan
Co. C. Fifth Regiment
Minnesota Vols
Commanding Post

This dispatch had to get through. Sheehan sent it with Jack Frazer, a half-breed scout and hunter, over 60 years of age but tougher than most half that mark, and an old friend of Henry Sibley. The Sioux knew him as "Iron Face". It looked made of iron as he set off on the post's last horse through what had become a lightning-streaked downpour to reach the capital, 100 miles distant.

Uttering a short prayer for the success of his rider's mission, the Lieutenant issued orders for an assembly on the parade grounds in two hours time, hoping that the rain would moderate during that period.

Rumors flew during that interim, which the commander undertook to squelch when, after doubling the guard, he climbed up on his flagpole-perch to speak.

"Two hours ago", he shouted, "I sent a courier directly to the Governor seeking reinforcements. This follows one sent yesterday. At least one of them will get through. Reinforcements could come at any time, but we need to respond to our situation as if they were *not* to come.

"I am proud of your actions to date. There was a battle yesterday, and *we won*. We learned something about Little Crow's tactics that will be helpful to us, but he also learned about ours, our strengths and our weaknesses. Our first weakness was our failure to see his initial actions as a diversion, That allowed our eastern flank to be attacked almost undefended. Our second weakness was to *waste* our ammunition trying to match their firepower. We can't, we shouldn't and we won't. Let them run out if they wish. We will fire to kill, not to frighten! We will pick our targets, and conserve our ammunition if we can't see one.

"I want you to return to your positions. I want you to re-*look* at your positions. A couple of feet in one direction or another could give you a better view of a hiding place. Make sure your fields of view – and of fire – overlap. The Sioux Indian in battle lives on surprise. We need to take it away from him.

"We did it once. We can do it again, and again if need be. Be alert. Be careful. If I get word regarding reinforcements, you'll know. In the meantime, we are *it*. Act accordingly"

Jumping down from his platform, Sheehan noted that there were no cheers from the grim-faced crowd surrounding him. He had no intention of allowing his fighters to sit around contemplating their future. Immediately he assigned four civilians to digging a well within the compound for use in the event of a long-term siege. With the supply of musket balls running low, Sgt. Jones organized a group of walking-wounded to collect the spent balls fired by the attackers, and to cut nails for use as bullets. These killed as effectively as bullets in a direct hit, and produced a shrieking sound that appeared to unnerve the Indians. There appeared to be an ample supply of spherical case shot for the cannon, so Jones ordered a supply to be taken to the women in the barracks, where they were disassembled, and the shot converted to rifle bullets.

While the garrison, out of communication with the outside world, prepared for a longer siege, there was a flurry of telegraphic communication between potential rescuers. From the governor:

To the People of Minnesota:

The Sioux Indians on our western frontier have risen in large bodies, attacked the settlements, and are murdering men, women and children. The rising appears concerted and extends from Fort Ripley to the southern boundary of the state. In this extremity I call upon the militia of the Valley of the Minnesota and the outside counties adjoining the frontier, to take horses and arm and equip themselves, taking with them subsistence for a few days, and at once report, separately or in squads, to the officer commanding the expedition now moving up the Minnesota River to the scene of the hostilities.

Alexander Ramsey
Executive Chamber
St. Paul, Aug. 21, 1862

Hon. E. M. Stanton
Secretary of War

    The Sioux Indians on our western border have risen, and are murdering men, women and children. I have ordered a party of men out, Under Co. H. H. Sibley, and given the command of the Sixth Regiment, also ordered up, to Capt. A. A Nelson, U. S. Army. I must have Nelson. Telegraph at once.

                                  Alex. Ramsey

Hon. C.E. Flandreau
St. Peter or New Ulm

    My Dear Sir: I have just received your note of yesterday. I leave with 225 men for St. Peter tomorrow evening, and hope to be there by 3 or 4 o'clock, from which point I will be directed in my movements by latest intelligence. News just received here, whether true or false, state (sic) that either the fort or the outbuildings were burned last night. Don't expose yourself to attack by an overwhelming force before I unite forces with you.

                                Col. H.H. Sibley

Brigadier General Schofield
St. Louis, Mo.

    Send the Third Regiment Minnesota Volunteers against the Indians on the frontier of Minnesota.

                            H. W. Halleck
                            General-In-Chief
                            War Department
                            Washington, Aug. 22, 1862

    As the nation's top military officer was directing a full regiment to the relief of the besieged settlers, the defenders of Ft. Ridgely were aware only of the actions occurring before them. The intent of those actions became clear that same afternoon.

>*About 1 clock PM Indians appeared in sight were all mounted on horse back (sic) until they got within ½ mile of garrison where they dismounted sounded the war whoop and broke into yells of defiance It appeared to me as though the gates of hell were broken open and all the firy (sic) dragons of its bottomless pits were approaching a little band of brave but exhausted soldiers at 12 oclk the Indians surrounded the garrison on three sides   commenced firing volley after volly (sic) until dark   Indians attempted to rush into garrison with warclubs and tomahawks at 4 different times during the afternoon but were met with canister and shell   paralyzing them which caused them to fall back every time   I saw a shot fired by ordnance Sergeant Jones from a 5 pound gun which elevated some of them in the air   still they would persist and charge with fury. I had soldiers in garrison well protected by the breastworks which we had build (sic) previous to this days fight which caused but few casualties   one killed and three wounded   one man killed belonging to the Renville Rangers   Sergeant Blackmer of Co. C Shot through the face, private Andrew Luther Co C wounded in the thigh   and so ends the contest between 700 Indians and a small band of 125 soldiers who held the fort.*
>
>   *T.J. Sheehan Journal*
>   *August 22, 1862*

    The young lookout was the first to spot them. He'd been high atop the now-empty ammunition magazine scanning the western perimeter from south to north. He had simply raised his hand while peering through the 'scope, and stayed in that position for a full minute, by which time this silent gesture had commanded the attention of virtually everyone in the compound. He turned and leaped from the nearly 6' height of the shed onto the mud below, running back into the compound while shouting "Shit, sir! Oh, shit! Here they come, here they *really* come!"

CHAPTER THIRTY FIVE

Sheehan, who'd begun walking out to the lookout's post after sighting the boy's upraised arm, now sprinted to meet the terrified youth. Grabbing he telescope and waving the breathless lad back to the compound, he climbed up the pallet propped against the shack's eastern wall and hastily scanned the horizon through the powerful glass.

Turning, he shouted "Lt. Gere! Company! To your posts!".

After noting the young officer scrambling to comply, Sheehan took a deep breath and took in the scene spreading out before him on the horizon.

Little Crow had had two days to think about his failed attempt to capture the fort. Though the number remained unknown, his casualties had to have been substantial. He had underestimated the firepower in the fort. It was unlikely he would make that mistake again. Following that failure, and that at New Ulm, the taking of Ft. Ridgely had become an obsession with him. He justified his previous poor showing because of the lack of support from the two war chiefs who had, in his opinion, *tricked* him into leading the uprising in the first place. Shakopee and Red Middle Voice had shunned the hard fighting in favor of raping and raiding south and west of their camp.

No more, said Little Crow. Killing the soldiers was their only chance for overall victory. He had entered a war for territory, they for revenge. But even revenge had gone too far. Surely the Great Father would now seek revenge of his own. Their only hope now was to annihilate the soldiers at the fort, quickly drive the then-defenseless settlers from the area, and use the territory seized as the only bargaining chip available when the whites came at them with the big guns and legions of troops that stretched beyond the horizon. The fort *must* fall, and it must do so while Taoyateduta maintained whatever control he could muster over his still rabid raiders. To him, that meant *today*.

He had called for members of the Rice Creek soldiers' lodge, demanding that they seek out the two chiefs and order them to return to his camp immediately. He had sent runners to the Upper Sioux, the Wahpeton and Sisseton Dakota, many of whom had finally joined him in the raiding. In the space of little more than a single day, his elegance had brought together the once mighty Sioux for the one great battle that would rid his land of the cursed whites once and for all.

The picture this force produced made Sheehan's mouth go dry. There were no fewer than 700 warriors approaching from the west, led by Little Crow in an elegant horse-drawn buggy commandeered from David Faribault, a mixed-blood prisoner. Maybe there were more. The column went to 4- and 5-wide, stretching more than a mile behind the chief. Most of the warriors were mounted. There were the Mdewanketons, over 100 of Shakopee and Red Middle Voice's fighters, though still neither of their war chiefs. Nearly 300 of the Upper Sioux had joined the column, and over 100 former farmer Indians who had swapped their white man's garb for breechcloths and body paint, their hoes for tomahawks, knives and shotguns. Many of these, it was later learned, were there under death threat from Little Crow's marauders. There were over a dozen empty wagons, transportation for the pillage they clearly intended to collect. Women and children accompanied the column, clutching spare ponies for the warriors. No Sioux army of this strength had ever been gathered in the lives of its members this day. It was a giddy experience for most, surely a predictor of ultimate victory.

His vision blurred by his slightly trembling hands, Sheehan could see the laughter and the light-hearted prodding among leading members of the column. Here a garishly-painted raider shoved his double-barreled shotgun at the head of his companion. There a bow came crashing down on the rump of the horse ahead, spilling its rider to the ground. To these savages, most of whom had not been in the group defeated two days earlier, this was a celebration, a *game* in which the scoring was taken in gruesome measure.

Winning, for Sheehan, was not to *repulse* a massed attack, an unlikely result given the relative size of their forces, but to *prevent* it from happening in the first place. To succeed, to save the fort and its occupants, he must turn his defense into an active attack on the attackers, to diffuse their charges and make their goal not worth the risks it entailed.

The Lieutenant went to one knee, silently intoning a prayer, then said "Thy will be done", rose, scrambled down the pallet and trotted back to what he hoped was the security of the garrison. It was time for business.

By his brazen approach, with no attempt to hide, Little Crow appeared to be trying to sow fear among the defenders, but this time there was no confusion, no panic in the fort. There was some whistling, and the normal "butterflies" that usually accompany contests of almost any kind. These were largely settled when some joker suggested that the "bad shots" be put up in front, since there were so many targets that *no one* could miss. It was gallows humor, but had a positive effect on the shooters who *were* up front.

"Wait 'till you have a target, lads.", Sheehan repeated softly as he roamed back and forth along the western perimeter. He'd sent Lt. Gere to the eastern side to offer the same message, and reinforce the need to watch for sneak attacks from the arroyos.

Many of the oncoming raiders jumped from their horses and grabbed grass and goldenrod, and leaves from the trees to decorate their headbands. These would be normal proceedings for an ambush, disguising the bearer as he crawled through the grass. Why they were resorted to before what appeared to be an all-out frontal assault was anybody's guess.

Little Crow's plan was simple enough. Big Eagle later called it a "grand affair". Use the massive force of his warriors to either overwhelm the defenders from the start, or cause them to exhaust their ammunition during the initial charges and become victims of Mankato's massed assault later on. They would attack from all four sides at once. As for the big guns, Little Crow had convinced his men that because the guns were awkward and could only fire in one direction at a time, and the Indians could fire *at* them from every direction at once, that the guns would soon be silenced – or taken over by the Indians and turned against the defenders. To sweeten the pot, he said he would personally bestow an eagle tail-feather on anyone who killed a man at the wagon-guns.

The post's defenses had been shored up as well as possible. Everything movable that was capable of deflecting an enemy missile had been used to fortify the barriers between buildings. The best marksmen had been placed on the roofs or second stories of the buildings. Dirt from the now 4-5' deep trenches had strengthened the barriers above, and provided cover for those standing behind. Some men lay prone, shooting at ground level from behind upended tables and wagons, while others fired from directly above them. Portholes had been established in the defenses wherever possible. Powder and balls – both collected from previous assaults and taken from spherical case shot – had been distributed and appeared to be in ample supply if carefully used.

"Have a target!", Sheehan had said.

Dirt had been shoveled onto the roofs, combining with the dampness to thwart fire from arrows. Water barrels had been placed strategically throughout the compound, and each person had a cup.

Defense from today's assault would largely depend on the big guns, Sheehan knew. The biggest, a massive 24-pounder, was brought out with some effort and placed in the gap between the commissary and the officers' quarters, facing west. Mr. Whipple manned his gun in the northeast corner, Sgt. McGrew faced northwest, and Sgt. Jones put himself in the southeast quadrant, overlooking the ravine that had given the Indians such cover during the last attack.

Just before the attack Joe Courselle's wife gave birth to a stillborn, which he immediately buried in a small box and returned to his position on the barrier. Mrs. Courselle's sobs echoed through the nearly silent compound as the defenders crouched in wait for the attackers.

It took concentration for the defenders of each direction to look only in that direction as they noticed themselves being surrounded. The warriors had left their horses a good ¾ mile distant, with their wagons, women and children. The "family affair" nature of these assaults was eerie to most of the defenders. Families of armed primitives trying to wrench their world back to the dark ages, and the fort foursquare in the way.

CHAPTER THIRTY SIX

The assault this time started with a single arrow thudding into the ground just feet from where Lt. Sheehan and Lt. Gere were standing near the flagpole, followed by a literal shower of fire arrows. Other than keeping the defenders' heads down, the arrows had no effect. The demoniac yells of the attacking Sioux definitely did. It was a sound unlike any other, a trilling shriek that assaulted the eardrum when uttered by a single warrior, and drowned out all thought when repeated by hundreds simultaneously.

The roar of the post's big guns softened the impact of those shrieks, now peppered with American curse words as the raiders grew closer.

Once again the bullets of the enemy fell with the volume of a Minnesota hailstorm, embedding in the wooden and mud structures and falling to the ground inches deep against the stone barracks. The defenders' return fire added to the continuous roar, punctuated at intervals by the earthshaking boom of the big guns from all four quarters

While helping trooper John Able replace a firing pin, Sheehan noticed a group of eastern – perimeter defenders mounting bayonets to meet a half-dozen warriors less than 50 feet distant. Wondering how the raiders had managed to get so close, he and the private were able to commandeer a just-charged 12-pound Napoleon gun and bring it to bear on the Indians at virtually point-blank range. When the smoke cleared, three of the attackers lay writhing on the ground; the others were nowhere to be seen.

The firing continued on all sides for what seemed like days, but continued in fact for less than two hours. It was during this time that Sheehan perfected the running crouch that he used to patrol the perimeter and demonstrate that the fort's command structure was still in place. He did not feel in danger of being hit by an *intentional* shot because of the thick smoke that engulfed the garrison. Astonishingly, though he estimated that as many as 1000 rounds had been fired at the compound, *no one was hit.*

After this first assault, it seemed that both sides needed to take a breath. The firing on the Indian side gradually subsided, followed by that of the fort's defenders. The raiders withdrew across the western prairie, and back down the arroyos. It was a brief respite, but a valuable one. Men drank, pissed where they stood, dipped kerchiefs into water barrels, splashed themselves and attempted to gather breaths of fresh air through the wet cloth. Water was poured over the barrels of nearly red-hot rifles, the guns hissing like angry cats. Two citizens set about carving balls from the mud and wood structures, and sorting out the piles beneath the stone barracks to find those still round. These were hastily distributed. Mrs. Muller came out from the improvised hospital to gather the wounded herself, only to gratefully discover that there were none.

That's when the "plinking" began.

This was a fire-phase, not an all out physical assault. From all sides, rounds came pinging into the fort. The volume was a fraction of the rifle thunder of the previous hours, but sufficient to keep the defenders from standing or walking about, and definitely having an effect on morale. When it appeared that the firing was to be ongoing, one of the civilian defenders in the southeast quadrant muttered a colorful curse. Moments later another curse rang out, followed by a string of foul language issued by one of the cannoneers at the northeast 5-pounder. At that point, the swearing became general, first out of honest frustration and anger, then of an almost hysterical nature, all sides trying to outdo others in the sincerity and/or creativity of their invective, while dissolving into gales of long-repressed laughter. Unfortunately, the tension-busting fun wasn't to last long.

The spasmodic rifle fire proved to be part of Little Crow's plan, one not shared with the warriors whose victory he had assured. Once again the idea was to draw the fire of those in the fort, exhaust their will and their supplies, then produce the final victory with a massed assault led by Mankato from the southwest ravine. Two miscalculations disrupted the chief's plan. First, though Little Crow had assured an easy victory, those assurances did not result in his forces abandoning cover during the initial assault. Had the Indians provided ready targets, they may well have drawn fire from the fort and depleted ammunition supplies. The raiders, however, did *not* provide easy targets, and the fort's ammunition stock remained healthy.

Second, Little Crow's assessment of the clumsiness of the big guns was not based on fact. In the hands of a skilled crew, a 12-pounder could be handled with nearly the agility of one of the heavy rifles of the day. Marauders approaching the back of a big gun site without fear of retribution usually found their plans – and often their lives – upended.

The warriors did what they could. Outbuildings to the southwest – the root house, ice house, suttler's warehouse and granary – were easily occupied by the raiders, a strategy that successfully lured them into those fragile structures, which were then blown away by focused cannon fire. The one negative: the smoke from the ensuing fires combined with that from woodpile and hay fires set by Mankato's men to lay down a blanket so thick and hazy that it allowed braves to get within 100 feet of the parade ground. A pair of cannon canisters and a burst of rifle fire disbursed the band that did, however.

The approach of the group from the southwest had the effect of focusing attention on that quarter. Spotters had been aware that raiders had been entering the ravine there for a time, but now they were encountering a much higher volume than had been suspected. In the space of 20 minutes, civilian teamster Eric Dreyfuss counted 96 "red devils" entering the ravine. While wary of the Indians' intentions – a ruse? – Sheehan ordered massive firepower to the quadrant in anticipation of a massed attack. Of the six cannon available, Sgt. Jones wheeled two 12-pounders and the 24-pound monster around to meet such a charge, the 24-pounder loaded with a double-charge of canister shot. Adding to this concentrated firepower, the commander ordered five of the marksmen manning the 2nd floor of the barracks building to be sent to the southwest barrier, which they did with barrel rests for their guns, ample ammunition and, in the case of three of them, their own personal loaders. Four of the five carried handguns as well. In all, there were three cannon and approximately 60 by-now-hardened defenders in the southwest quadrant when someone gave a signal and the Indian raiders began pouring from the ravine.

To the squinted eye, it must have looked like a copper river flowing uphill; there appeared to have been hundreds of the warriors in the arroyo, now streaming through the cleft looking to kill.

But the warrior force faced two disadvantages. Following literally on the heels of one another, they could not shoot until they were clear of the men before them, and since none took to the ground, their actual firepower was substantially less than their number might indicate. The second is that coming from the lip of the ravine they were necessarily a compressed group, with only 4 or 5 able to crest the ridge at once. This enabled gunners to pour intense fire into an area less than ten feet across, with the result that most of those who emerged early on soon fell, to be clambered over by those following.

Many of those who did make it through fled immediately to the west along the southern edge of the barrier, creating active targets while seeking shelter in the burned-out outbuildings, or dropping back down from the edge of the bluff.

As the flow of raiders continued in spite of the carnage produced by concentrated small-arms fire, the two 12-pounders opened up, taking a number of victims and momentarily plugging the flow. Then, in what appeared to be a suicidal charge, several dozen of the raiders attempted to simultaneously breech the crest of the ravine *and* both sides closer to the top. This effort, bold or insane, was met with a single blast from the double-charged 24-pounder that reverberated across the entire battlefield, lifted several attackers off the ground and flung them back into the gully, and cut two more to ribbons with its projected shrapnel. The result was that this area of attack closed. It had lasted for less than a quarter of an hour, resulting in massive casualties to the attackers, and none to the defenders.

During this assault, Little Crow had positioned himself to the southeast of the compound. When he saw the devastation being wrought on his warriors, he called them back and ordered an attack on the northeast quadrant, *before* the big guns could be repositioned. But again he erred, thinking that the volume of cannon-fire must have indicated that all were employed at the southwest corner. In fact three remained. One, effectively manned by Mr. Whipple and covered by Lt. Gere's sharpshooters, met the new assault by lowering its barrel and sending two terrifying rounds through the massed assailants. Coupled with Gere's fusillade, the concentration of firepower sent the savages back into the trees, placing the fort nearly out of range of the Indian long guns.

    Adding a dash of bravado, Mr. Whipple lowered his barrel even further, and sent a round skipping off in the direction now occupied by Little Crow. It proved to be more than a rude and unlucky omen to the fuming field commander. While not a direct hit, the shell burst within a dozen yards of his hiding place, and pieces of shrapnel struck him glancing blows about the head. Though no blood was drawn, the chief lay dazed for several moments, and had to be helped from the field by nearby warriors. The fact that he'd been hit spread among his band in minutes, and brought a temporary halt to their charges. Word of the ambitious and accurate exercise with the "clumsy" cannon brought shrieks of delight from defenders who witnessed the event.

    The joy was to be short-lived. Within a half-hour, word that the leader had survived the cannon shot brought him new adulation, and renewed frenzy on the part of the warrior body that had until then been torn apart by the post's aggressive defense. Directing the warriors who had survived the charge from the southwest ravine to the northwest corner, Little Crow had them describe a massive arc along the western perimeter, just outside rifle range. Another large column was seen running up the eastern barrier, intending to cross over the northern perimeter and join up for a charge on the fort's least-barricaded quadrant.

Both the north and west, however, were essentially treeless, and afforded the greatest visibility of the raiders' maneuvers. Sgt McGrew, rather than exhibiting concern over the coming attack, appeared giddy at the Indians' movements.

"It's an opportunity, sir", he said to Lt. Sheehan through a face-creasing grin. "The bastards were looking for a slaughter, were they? Well then let's give it to 'em".

Employing his crews and some of Lt. Gere's men from Company C, he wheeled a pair of 12-pounders and the once-again double-charged 24-pounder to focus fire on what he projected to be the meeting place of the two warrior columns. And then, while most of the quadrant's defenders grew nervous at the size of the gathering force, McGrew and his men dawdled. Only after the better part of a half-hour was the wisdom of his patience exhibited.

"Let the mutts work themselves into a bit of a frenzy", the Sergeant said. "When we yank the legs out from under 'em it'll make it all the more memorable. *Damned* if they'll be so anxious after that".

When the combined force turned toward the fort, less than a couple of hundred yards distant, and began their trilling war cries and waving their weapons in the air, Mcgrew let loose with all three weapons at once.

The ground literally shook. Even the defenders who had not been part of this last-minute planning turned with looks of horror on their faces, thinking that the post's ammunition supplies had just exploded. It was a deafening, multiple "B-O-O-MMMM", that reverberated in the thick, damp air. The shells and the shrapnel cut through the massed warriors with ghastly effect, leaving a gaping hole in their number. Under the staccato fire of the troops who had rushed to this corner, the focus of the native survivors turned immediately from charging the fort to hauling away their wounded, and finding some sort of cover. Their dead were left on the field.

CHAPTER THIRTY SEVEN

The Sioux force under Little Crow had been operating on rage, seasoned with hope. Those, particularly the elders, who had had opportunities to visit the major cities and witness the endless multitudes and the power of those who build buildings, and railroads, and guns that sound like thunder and kill from a mile away, knew in their hearts that their uprising was both righteous and foolish. They had been willing to begin it, to give themselves the opportunity to produce small victories, and to let those victories provide them with encouragement. With that encouragement they would have gone on. The Winnebago would have joined, and the Chippewa.

But there were no victories. The proudest native force on the upper Mississippi had been reduced to looting and raping and the slaughter of innocents. Could not the mightiest assembly of warriors seen in the memories of the elders not whip a village of farmers and seamstresses and clerks? Or a fort without walls manned by a handful of frightened amateur troops who had yet to shave?

Little Crow had been the man to follow given his ability to assemble the bands. But who had given away Sioux lands in treaty after treaty? And though he had fought individuals, what did he know of *war*? Little, as it turned out. He could scratch a plan in the dirt, but knew nothing of adjusting the second part given how the first had turned out. He was rigid, full of himself. He looked, but did not see, listened, but did not hear. He led from the *side*, too willing to test his theories with the flesh of his brothers. Those theories had now cost nearly 100 Sioux lives, and soon the legions of blue-coated soldiers would descend on them to take hundreds more. He had challenged the Great Father. Now *all* would suffer.

    The marauders had left. Sheehan's first task was to count the dead and wounded. In all, three soldiers and four citizens were killed during the siege thus far, and 13 wounded. As the smoke lifted, lookouts were sent to what remained of the outbuildings, with orders to watch for enemy dead who might in fact just be wounded. The lookouts were authorized to kill them. The firing had ceased late in the afternoon, and the remaining daylight hours were used for resupplying those manning the barriers – ammunition, food, water and "subs", young civilians who substituted their eyesight for that of the shooters while the latter answered nature's call.

    The mood in the fort was temporarily jubilant, settling as the hours passed to a kind of hopeful determination. Time and time again they'd been tested by the savages, and had beaten them off. Each time they'd discovered holes in their defenses, and filled them. Now the fort had what could be described as real walls, at least in their ability to divert Indian rifle or shotgun fire. The bows had been used mostly to shoot fire arrows, and even that had stopped given the dampness of the roofs and the mud that had been placed there. The defenders had become used to their one-meal-a-day regimen, and though they didn't like it were able to fake full bellies with crackers and water, of which there was plenty. Ammunition supplies appeared to be holding. The cannoneers had achieved the status of folk heroes, with Jones, McGrew and Whipple on a platform of their own.

    The shooters kept up their 4-hour sleeping shifts, often in unimaginable positions with heads on pails, seated in leaning chairs or kneeling draped over empty water barrels. No one knew when Sheehan slept, given his and Gere's omnipresence at the walls and among the refugees. In spite of their youth, both officers projected a level of calm that translated into confidence among the observers, and served the garrison well during the length of the siege.

There was movement outside the fort that first night. Later it was determined that several warriors had returned to remove their dead. This they accomplished without launching new attacks, and none were directed at them. At no time during the siege did the Sioux initiate fighting during the night.

CHAPTER THIRTY EIGHT

Dawn on the 23rd cast a dull, syrupy light on a cadre of wilted defenders. For most, hours of sleep could be measured in single digits over the past four nights. Heat, humidity and the incessant, pricky whining of clouds of mosquitoes were taking their toll, as were the flies attracted by overflowing sanitary facilities. What had been terrifying but intensely involving had shifted into a dreary and ominous marking of time. The officers and sergeants made their usual rounds, offering encouragement and handing out rods and oily patches to keep the shooters' weapons serviceable, but some of the civilians, silent, challenged Sheehan with their grim expressions, as if the whole affair was *his* fault.

Though radiating confidence during his rounds, Sheehan's expression, too, was grim during his meetings in Captain Marsh's quarters with Lt. Gere and the sergeants. Now that no direct attack was underway, there was time to contemplate what course would or could be followed in the next hours or days. The rationing of food, water, even ammunition had been based on the probability of relief within several days. But though a number of couriers had been dispatched with urgent pleas for reinforcements, there had been no word from the outside world – and no certain knowledge that any of them had gotten through.

Even without the constant threat of massacre, living conditions in the compound were deteriorating. The elderly and wounded were becoming weaker by the day. More of the children were crying continually. Several of the men were coughing up bloody phlegm from hours of ingesting gunpowder and smoke. The compound was so crowded it was difficult to move without stepping on or over someone, and the protests of those stepped on were growing more vigorous. Among those at the barricades tempers frayed and accusations began to flow. Mr. Blackett was shooting in the air. 15-year old Gunther shot for noise, and was wasting ammunition. Mrs. Watkins wanted the soldiers to turn around when she used the privy. Burly Rev. Jared didn't lift a stick when the barriers were being built. Some of the civilians grumbled that the military was supposed to get them out of this, and why weren't they? The troopers began to resent the whining of the settlers. And outside the fort, only glimpses of an increasingly furtive enemy.

Saw several Indians expected a fight we were all ready for them but they did not attack the fort and proceeded to New Ulm or rather in that direction 3 or 400 in the fort we were digging entrenchments all the time making the fort secure against attack in case of more Indian reinforcements thus passed the time.
TJ Sheehan Journal
August 23, 1862

All comparatively quiet a few Indians insight a few shots fired by them over the garrison saw one Indian sticking up his blanket for the soldier to shoot at I was informed of an Indian being there and saw the treachery of his actions and killed him myself.
TJ Sheehan Journal
August 24, 1862

The Indians returned went by garrison in plain sight had plunder with them Oxen carts, etc. I think they had some prisoners with them they did not come to attack us and therefore there was nothing of importance in the way of occurrences about the fort comparatively still.

TJ Sheehan Journal
August 25, 1862

A number of Indians in sight all in fort having suspicion of attack and everyone alert and prepared for another encounter with them always intended to do them justice which they had administered to the Indians on previous occasions but they did not trouble us and the day passed in expectations and eager hopes for reinforcement.

TJ Sheehan Journal
August 26, 1862

*Indian spies assembled around nolls (*sic*) did not come close to the garrison had 40 men to work all night building breastworks and preparing for an expected attack the next day Co. McPhale arrived with reinforcements of about 300 horse men loud cheering in garrison felt much relieved and joyful of being reinforced Had not heard from abroad for eleven days except from refugees who had been driven from their homes by the Indians and would always try to approach the garrison by traveling at night and telling most thrilling accounts of the murders which had been committed by the Indians.*

TJ Sheehan Journal
August 27, 1862

The four nights of hide-and-seek with Little Crow's warriors had left the fort's defenders with itchy trigger fingers and increasingly glum outlooks. Bets were cast not about whether an attack would occur, but when. A flurry of firing occurred just before daylight at what turned out to be an emaciated coyote and her two pups loping toward the river just outside the western perimeter. No one slept that night with the racket of the detail Sheehan had ordered to further shore up the post's defenses with any solid object that could be transported to the barriers. Those attempting sleep in the barracks were politely requested to rise, then the bunks beneath them were removed and added to the "wall". All doors that had not been previously removed were noisily appropriated, as were their frames, even the frames of the windows.

"We don't expect to be here in winter", the droll Sheehan explained.

It was well into the day and breastwork-building efforts were still underway when a woman peering out of the now windowless 2nd story of the barracks building screamed "Riders!", and the post once again erupted in turmoil. But within the space of a single minute terror turned into ecstasy when she yelled "It's all right! They're *ours!* It's us. They're *ours!*".

Eyes ran and guns were discharged in the air as the end of the siege presented itself in the form of Lieutenant Colonel Samuel McPhail and nearly 200 mounted troopers and volunteers. Under a flapping American flag the contingent cantered up to the northeast corner of the compound, reined up, and for what seemed like five full minutes basked in the applause and cheers being bestowed on them by the subjects of their rescue.

By this time Lieutenants Sheehan and Gere had arrived on the scene - Sheehan having stopped by Captain Marsh's quarters to button his shirt and acquire his hat – and pushed through the cavorting crowd.

Leaning forward in his stirrups and trying to keep his now skittish horse under control, the Colonel suppressed a broad grin, saluted sharply, and said: "Col.

McPhail reporting for duty, Lieutenant. Might we come in?".

CHAPTER THIRTY NINE

Smartly returning his salute, and *not* trying to suppress his grin, Sheehan replied "You damn right --- sir!", and began tearing down the barricade himself. Seconds later, half-a-hundred helping hands had produced a 40-foot-wide gap in the suddenly less-critical barrier, and a stream of human- and horse-flesh rolled through to a gauntlet of adulation that included grown men jumping around like kids who'd just tipped over the outhouse, and women trying to hug their horses. The miracle was that no one got shot or trampled.

It was fully an hour before the commotion died down, and it was determined that the bulk of the new arrivals would have to bivouac outside the compound. There just wasn't enough room for what now surpassed 500 humans and a couple hundred horses inside an area a good man could throw a stone across. Most of the riders concurred. They weren't about to picket their horses away from themselves, where they could be run off by a pack of painted red jackals.

By nightfall, a semblance of order had been restored, and most of the rescued and the rescuers settled down together with meager but welcome rations from the post's now almost depleted supply. Then the officers and non-coms retired to Captain Marsh's quarters to exchange intelligence on what had been happening to both groups.

Captain Marsh had been wrong. While the uprising was not general, it did involve a good portion of the young warriors from the start, and was even now spreading among the "wait and see" factions among the Sioux, and beginning to draw in the Winnebagoes and even, some said, the Sioux's traditional enemy, the Chippewa (Ojibway). Had the post fallen, it is likely those tribes would have joined the uprising, and devastated the entire southern half of the state. The absence of relief for so long a time wasn't because no one knew that the post was under siege, McPhail said, but because of the need to fend off other attacks, negotiate with the bureaucracy, and, in at least one instance, deal with an extreme level of caution on the part of a troop commander.

Governor Ramsey had received the dispatch sent by Gere on August 19. He had immediately ridden to Ft. Snelling to assess troop levels, and determine how many of those training for duty in the south could be diverted to Ft. Ridgely. His initial appraisal was that four companies were sufficiently trained and equipped to do so. His next task was to recruit a commander for the brigade, which he found in Henry H. Sibley. Sibley was a friend and former political rival of Ramsey's, and had been Minnesota's first governor beginning with statehood four years earlier. He also had been a resident for 28 years, and a fur-trader with the Sioux for that entire period. He had no military experience, but certainly had command experience as a governor, and knew well the Sioux country, language and customs. If not the perfect choice for such an assignment, he appeared a good one at the moment.

But Henry Sibley proved to be a thorough man, if not necessarily a bold one. His strength appeared to be logistics. The monitoring and maintenance of supplies for the mission appeared to have *become* the mission for the new commander. He did not appear to approach risk with any enthusiasm, an unfortunate characteristic for those charged with rescuing others currently undergoing life-threatening risk.

Sibley's first assignment as commander was to lead his four companies to the rescue of Ft. Ridgely, picking up supplies on the way. The four companies were infantry, not cavalry, thus all movement was to be accomplished on foot. By the end of the second day, August 21, he and his command had reached St. Peter, an admirable accomplishment for a 48-hour span. It seems to have been one of his last.

In St. Peter, he came upon his old hunting friend, Jack Frazer. Jack was one of two dispatch riders Sheehan had sent – out of seven – who had gotten through. Jack was a colorful character, capable of equally-colorful description. Unfortunately, after hearing Jack's colorful description of what was happening in and around the fort, Sibley decided then and there *not* to pick up supplies on the way, but to wait for them – and more reinforcements – right there in St. Peter, 90 miles from the siege.

While still feeling his way as a combat commander, Sibley proved to be an avid contributor to the flurry of telegraphic communications between those empowered with quelling the uprising, beginning with his first day on the job.

His Exellency(sic), ALEX. RAMSEY,
St. Paul, Minn.,
Sir: I have the honor to report that the steamer Pomeroy has arrived here, with, however, but a portion of the fixed ammunition required, and without tents or camping equipage of any kind.

The men detailed for the expedition are now on board, ready for departure. I shall proceed to Shakopee with them, and endeavor to prepare transportation so as to be ready to move as soon as my quartermaster, Mr. Mills, shall have secured the articles above mentioned and other requisites, and rejoined me with them.

> *The men are without cooked rations, and I trust no time will be lost in having all of these articles furnished, as they are necessary, not only to the comfort of the men, but to the success of the expedition.*
>
> *Very respectfully, your obedient servant,*
> *H.H. Sibley*
> *Colonel, Commanding*

The governor, in the meanwhile, had issued a call to militias from the Minnesota River Valley and counties adjoining the frontier to "*...take horses and arm and equip themselves, taking with them subsistence for a few days, and at once report, separately or in squads, to the officer commanding the expedition now moving up the Minnesota River to the scene of the hostilities...This outbreak must be suppressed, and in such manner as will ever prevent its repetition...*".

A day earlier, August 26, Sibley had finally determined that he'd assembled a force large enough – 1600 men – and well-equipped enough to engage the enemy, and had started moving toward the fort. That movement had been spotted by Little Crow's spies, and word quickly sent to his camp at the Lower Sioux Agency. His old friend and hunting partner, the Long Trader, was coming after him. Immediately, Little Crow assembled the entire population of the Agency – still some 3000 Indians awaiting their annuity money – and set off with his 250 white and mixed-blood prisoners to escape the onslaught he knew would surely be coming.

At the same time, his rage at failing to secure the involvement of his brothers at the Upper Agency – Sissetons and Wahpetons – grew to the point of breaking, and he dispatched several hundred of his braves to intimidate the group into participation. To his surprise and stark disappointment, the Upper Agency chiefs not only refused, but accused Little Crow and his leaders of insolence and arrogance, and turned them away with their own threats of violence.

Within hours, while the procession of Lower Agency Indian refugees fled the fighting, a council was held between the two groups, and eloquent arguments made both for releasing the captives and discontinuing the fighting, and for killing the captives, restoring the fighting, slaughtering the whites, and rejoining their British confederates of an earlier time. Soon it became obvious that neither side was going to persuade the other. The Upper Sioux chiefs put out a call for Sissetons and Wahpetons to come to their aid and protect them from the Lower Sioux warriors. Within a day, a force of some 300 was assembled, painted for war, ready to repel the Lower Sioux. The next day another standoff occurred between the two sides, the following day another.

It was enough. Little Crow, wearied now, discouraged, knowing that his only hope for victory was to be found in a united front, relented. He would continue the fight, but made no further attempt to recruit the Upper Agency "friendlies", who continued their efforts to free the white and mixed-blood prisoners.

This would have been welcome news to Col. Sibley, who arrived at Ft. Ridgely a day after Col. McPhail's troop with his "sufficient" force, and promptly set up an orderly tent village around the compound, from which he was not to move for several more days.

The fort having been secured with McPhail's arrival, Lt. Sheehan had formally turned its command over to him, and now awaited further orders.

CHAPTER FORTY

Now began a second war, a series of engagements in which Lt. Sheehan's role, and that of the remainder of his fellow defenders, would be limited. The first was a defensive conflict, with troopers and settlers alike seeking only to prevent mayhem on themselves, their families and charges. Little Crow's warriors, bolstered by the unleashing of primitive rage and the element of surprise, held the bloody edge in the initial engagements, massacring the innocent and the unarmed without opposition until confronted by Ft. Ridgely. But their planning was equally primitive, confounded by poor communication, conflicting goals, the refusal to follow a common leader, the breadth of the battlefield, and the sporadic and undisciplined nature of their attacks. They would still kill, but the might of the military machine so feared by Little Crow was being assembled to confront them. Their role had been converted from pursuer to pursued, their time was limited, and the punishment they were to bring on their entire nation was severe beyond imagining.

The first step in this second war was a second debriefing session between Colonels Sibley and McPhail, and Lieutenants Sheehan and Gere. It began with the arrival of the former governor's forces and was once again held in Captain Marsh's quarters.

Sheehan had already spent considerable time lauding the performance of his subordinate, Lt. Gere, for his courage, diligence and ability to connect with both troopers and armed civilians during the siege. He had had no more sleep during the period than Sheehan himself, and had carried on his duties without hesitation, error or complaint.

Sheehan himself had been the subject of a stream of compliments by Col. McPhail the previous evening, during which the post's stores of spirituous beverages had been exhausted, more tears shed, and rank-free friendships developed.

This day, Wednesday, August 27, the mood was more business-like. Col. Sibley had promptly assumed command of the fort upon his arrival, and had cut short the ensuing celebration. His manner was curt, no-nonsense, and replete with references to his relationship to the current governor, Alexander Ramsey.

"I was first to hold that office", he told the assembled officers, "and I know what strain the governor must be under. But I've promised him we will soon have this madness under control, and by God, we will!"

The first order of business was to assess damage to the fort and its defenders. While the main compound of the fort itself looked storm-tossed, most of the damage to the structures was the result of their various panels and partitions having been ripped from their moorings to serve as barriers on the perimeter firing line. For the time being, the majority of these barriers were left in place. The status of the post's outbuildings was less encouraging; most had been voluntarily blasted apart by cannon shot to rob the invaders of places of concealment and protection from return fire.

The effectiveness of Sheehan's management of the post's defenses became evident in the casualty figures. Despite three concentrated assaults by up to an estimated 800 warriors, and days in between of native sniper fire, only 13 defenders had been wounded, and but three killed. Disbelieving, Col. Sibley ordered that these figures be corroborated, and only then congratulated Sheehan and Gere for their creative use of non-traditional defensive resources, and apparent exercise of "military principals and discipline". Sheehan rejected the credit, and asked that it go instead to his cannoneers and the perimeter gunners who had withstood the assaults with a combination of unshakeable courage and accurate fire. It was later determined that in excess of 100 of the attackers had perished.

Next came a summary of the assault's first day, some nine days earlier. First Lt. Gere was asked to describe the scene at the fort as the initial survivors began pouring in. The young officer recounted those events with a clarity that was startling, even to describing Captain Marsh's facial expressions as he received the victims' reports. Sibley seemed most interested in the captain's *mood* during these early hours, and how he responded to statements and signs that appeared cautionary. Col. Sibley had already shown himself to be a man opposed to what he considered to be rash action.

He sought specifics on the effects of the outbreak. How many victims had arrived at the fort. How many women? Children? Were they all from the Lower Agency? What kind of wounds had they sustained? Did the survivors think it was just a gang of rogue Indians? More? How many had guns? Did the captain appear to consider this information before deciding to go to the rescue? How many troops did he muster (47)? Had he asked for volunteers? How many troops was Lt. Gere left with to defend the fort (27)?

Sheehan felt compelled to call Sgt. John Bishop, one of Captain Marsh's survivors, to the briefing, to clarify both the military and humanitarian necessity of the captain's rescue attempt, and to answer the detailed questions that the colonel insisted on pursuing for nearly an additional hour. At the end of Bishop's testimony, Col. Sibley appeared satisfied that the military had not *started* the conflict, and that while the captain had blundered with his troops into an ambush, the urgency of his response and the need for immediate action would likely serve to exonerate him in the event of any future inquiry into the matter.

The colonel then spent the next several minutes explaining to the other three officers why it had taken so long for *him* to assist in the defense of Ft. Ridgley after being made aware of its circumstances in the dispatch received by Gov. Ramsey August 19. The others nodded, but made no comment.

During a pause, Sheehan, noting the massive size of the reinforcements surrounding the fort, and hoping for a response that would lead to easing his own physical exhaustion, asked simply, "Is it over?".

The two colonels looked at one another and then at the floor, realizing that Sheehan and his command had been beyond communication for fully eleven days.

"Hardly.", McPhail offered. "They tasted blood at the beginning, and it's sustained the thieving, murdering bastards ever since. They've practically leveled New Ulm. Good men dead. They're harassing Fort Abercrombie. The Chippewa have been massing around Ft. Ripley. 25 troopers killed and 13 wounded between Ridgely and those lost at the ferry. And *we* fight back. God only knows how many dead and maimed among those who can't. And it's not just *that* their killed; it's *how*. The newspapers are calling for every Indian to be either hung or booted out of the state, and from what I've seen you can't blame 'em."

The colonels continued to update Sheehan, Gere and Sgt. Bishop, who had been invited to stay, for much of the afternoon. The raids had had the effect of emptying most of southern Minnesota, from near St. Paul all the way to the border of Dakota Territory, an expanse of some 20,000 sq. miles. The Sioux had been ultimately driven off in all of their massed attacks, and had lost many men, but continued on their warpath against civilians and soldiers alike. At Birch Coulie they ambushed the party tasked with burying those already killed, as well as the force that had been sent to rescue them. At Wood Lake, a planned ambush of Sibley's larger force was foiled when troops out to steal potatoes almost ran over warriors hiding in the roadside brush, and the force was alerted. The Sioux lost 15 dead and many more wounded in this fight, that became the last major operation of the uprising.

  Dispirited, exhausted, and shunned by many of his own people for failing to turn their outrage into a return to their former glory, and certain of the gallows should he be caught, Taoyateduta, the Little Crow, slunk off to Dakota Territory, there to fail once again to bring outlying bands into what had become seen as his personal battle with the white population of the northwest frontier.

CHAPTER FORTY ONE

For the next three weeks, Lt. Sheehan served as on-site administrator of the effort to return Ft. Ridgley to some form of normalcy. Doors were re-hung, desks and bunks replaced, supplies ordered and inventoried, ditches filled, transportation for civilian survivors arranged, temporary barriers taken down, and construction on destroyed outbuildings begun. Lessons had been painfully learned about the defensibility of the post, and efforts were made to make it a fort in fact, as well as in name. Semi-permanent barriers were erected, shooting ports opened in perimeter buildings, thick wooden shutters installed, lookout posts erected, cannon pads of stone and cement laid down. The fort's original plans, calling for all stone structures, were brought out for review.

Though chafing at the orders that confined him to his current task, Sheehan, Gere and the remainder of Companies B and C were buoyed up by a rumor mill that buzzed with news of Union efforts in the Rebellion, including inferences that they would be joining that fray in the near future. And on September 18, 1862, Lt. Sheehan led his detachment of Company C back to Fort Ripley, to prepare for deployment to what was becoming known as the Civil War. Lt. Gere and the men of Company B left for Fort Snelling on November 9, as part of an escort under Col. W.R. Marshall, transferring a nearly two-mile-long column of sullen native captives to that fort. Within a matter of days after Gere's arrival, both companies left the Great Sioux Uprising and its aftermath behind, and proceeded south to hook up with their regiment near Oxford, Mississippi on December 12.

By now a hardened combat veteran, the 26-year-old officer approached his new posting with a mixture of anticipation and dread. He was no longer the fresh-faced town clerk, eager to give his life to the country that had been good to him. He had tasted hell already, and he knew he would be facing an enemy that was greater in number and firepower than anything he'd yet seen – and, from what he'd heard, nearly as vicious. But he brought with him to this real war a confident command that had faced the terrors of the past few months with guts and tenacity, and he looked forward to dishing a full measure of that out to the rebel forces they would soon meet.

CHAPTER FORTY TWO

September 9, 1862

The rationale for frustration and anger among the Santee Sioux could be argued. Their response to it could not. Public condemnation on the frontier was universal. While bands of mostly Lower Agency warriors were still on the run, in an address to the Minnesota Legislature Governor Alexander Ramsey left no room for negotiation with the murderers of innocents:

Our course then is plain. The Sioux Indians of Minnesota must be exterminated or driven forever beyond the borders of the state.

The public safety imperatively requires it. Justice calls for it. Humanity itself, outraged by their unutterable atrocities, demands it. The blood of the murdered cries to heaven for vengeance on these assassins of women and children. They have themselves made their annihilation an imperative social necessity. Faithless to solemn treaty obligations, to old friendships, to the ties of blood, regardless even of self-interest when it conflicts with their savage passions, incapable of honor, of truth, or of gratitude; amenable to no law; bound by no moral or social restraints – they have already destroyed in one monstrous act of perfidy, every pledge on which it was possible to found a hope of ultimate reconciliation.

They must be regarded and treated as outlaws. If any shall escape extinction, the wretched remnant must be driven beyond our borders and our frontier garrisoned with a force sufficient to forever prevent their return.

September 28, 1862

    Col. Sibley, at the head of an army nearing some 2000 men, was now actively arresting those among surrendered or captured Sioux suspected of being involved in the murder of innocents. Having experienced neither this nature nor volume of lawlessness, and not wishing to clog the civil justice system of southern Minnesota, he appointed a military commission of five officers to assess guilt and impose punishment. The five were Col. William Crooks of the Sixth Minnesota, Lieutenant Col. Marshall (soon replaced by Major George Bradley of the Seventh Minnesota), Captains Grant and Hiram S. Bailey of the Sixth regiment, and Lieutenant Rollin C. Olin of the Third regiment, who served as judge advocate.

    The commission met through November 3, during which time 393 cases were heard, resulting in 323 convictions and 303 sentences of death by hanging. The "trials" were quick; 16 were held that first day, resulting in 10 convictions. Just being involved in the battles merited a death sentence. When a brave offered a defense, prosecution witnesses were called. Whenever the defendants' and the witnesses' testimonies varied, the commission elected to believe that of the witnesses, and the defendant was condemned. Some trials were concluded in less than ten minutes.

    In part, the trials were publicly held to mollify a rage among the citizens even greater than that behind the uprising just over four months earlier. The area's newspapers carried the atrocities of the marauders on their front pages, helping to fuel citizen fury.
Threats issued verbally concerning the *probability* of vigilante justice moved from conversations between settlers to those same front pages. One example:

Rumor, double-tongued, brings to us much too frequently, words of doubt as to the fate of the red devils who have desolated our frontier. Shall we hold meetings and petition the president that justice be meted them? Nay! Let me tell you that I violate no secret when I say that all the Quakers this side of eternity cannot save a single red devil. If President Lincoln will not heed the petition that goes to him from five-hundred murdered whites, he will pay but little attention to the [earnest ministrations] of the living. So we of the frontier watch and wait. No matter how, nor when, but as sure as there is a living God, there will be a carnival of death, somewhere, among the Indians, even if from Washington come orders to let the miscreants loose.

Mankato Weekly Record
December 13, 1862

In the *St. Paul Union,* under the title *Charge of the Hemp Brigade,* a macabre poem summed up the mood of the populace:

Hemp on the throat of them,
Hemp round the neck of them,
Hemp under the ears of them,
    Twisting and choking;
Stormed at with shout and yell,
Grandly they'll hang and well,
Until the jaws of death,
Until the mouth of Hell
    Takes the three hundred

November 9, 1862

The 303 condemned prisoners were bundled up in wagons and hauled off to Mankato to await execution. In order to reach that city they were routed through New Ulm, where the attitude of the community was illustrated by the ferocity of the attacks against the bound Indians. Fist-sized rocks were rained down on the captives; buckets of human waste tossed from windows; boys with slingshots peppered the prisoners with stones and clumps of hardened horse dung; attempts were made to hijack individual wagons, or to lasso individuals and haul them off to be hung; shovels and bats and horsewhips were used to bash the prisoners, most of whom left the gauntlet bloodied and terrified of the rage they had produced among the white population.

In passing through the town of New Ulm, the long succession of wagons containing each ten prisoners, flanked by a strong force of mounted men, was set upon by a crowd of men, women and children, who showered brickbats and other missiles upon the shackled wretches, seriously injuring some fifteen of the latter and some of the guards. The assailants were finally driven back by a bayonet charge, and fifteen or twenty men who were among them were arrested and made to march on foot twelve miles to the spot where we camped for the night, where after being reprimanded for the insult to the U.S. flag committed by them and their female associates, they were released and compelled to walk back the entire distance to New Ulm. I did not dare to fire [into the crowd] for fear of killing women and children. The Dutch she-devils! They were as fierce as tigresses.

Letter from Col. Sibley to his wife

December 4, 1862
    A planned attack on the prison camp by several hundred armed local citizens was foiled by a ring of soldiers, nearly shoulder-to-shoulder, guarding the Indians.

December 6, 1862
    Issuance of the actual execution order for the 303 prisoners sentenced to die was left to President Lincoln, who had been besieged by compassionate easterners to commute the sentences of the poor primitives. Rumors to that effect found their way back to Minnesota, where *any* sign of compassion was roundly and publicly condemned by those who had suffered at the hands of the raiders. To consider the expressed and highly charged needs of both parties, the President assigned two clerks to review the records of the 303 in an effort to distinguish between those who had engaged in "normal" battle practices and those who had slaughtered the unarmed innocent. In the end, 39 of the prisoners were condemned to die, with the others remanded to custody.

December 20, 1862
    An article in the *Mankato Weekly Record* illustrates the community's response to Lincoln's rumored disposition of the remaining prisoners:

> *We protest against the pardon of these Indians....because if the President does not permit these executions to take place under the forms of law, the enraged people of Minnesota will dispose of these wretches without law. We do not wish to see mob law inaugurated in Minnesota, as it certainly will be if you force the people to it. We tremble at the approach of such a state of things in our State; you can give us peace*

or you can give us lawless violence. We pray you, sir, in view of all we have suffered, and of the dangers that still await us, LET THE LAW BE EXECUTED, LET JUSTICE BE DONE OUR PEOPLE.

With high respect, sir
M.S. Wilkinson
Cyrus Aldrich
Wm. Windom

December 17, 1862
Headquarters Indian Post
Mankato
SPECIAL ORDER NO. 11

  The President of the United States, having directed the execution of thirty nine of the Sioux and half-breed prisoners now in my charge, on Friday the 26th instant – he having postponed the time from the 19th instant – said execution will be carried into effect in front of the Indian prison at this place on that day at 10 O'clock A.M. The Executive also enjoins that no others of the prisoners be allowed to escape, and that they be protected for the future disposition of the government; and these orders will be executed by the military force at my disposal with the utmost fidelity. The aid of all good citizens is invoked, to maintain the law and constitutional authority of the land on that occasion. The State of Minnesota must not, in addition to the terrible wrongs and outrages inflicted upon her by murderous savages, suffer, if possible, still more fatally, in her prosperity and reputation, at the hands of a few of our misguided, though deeply injured, fellow-citizens.

STEPHEN MILLER
Col. 7th Min. Reg't Vols.,
Commanding Post

December 22, 1862
Headquarters Indian Post
Mankato
GENERAL ORDER NO. 18

All persons interested in Mankato, and the adjoining territory, for the distance of ten miles, from these Headquarters, are hereby notified to sell or give no intoxicating liquors of any description, including wine and beer, to the enlisted men of the United States forces in this valley or vicinity, unless it be upon an order from, or approved by the Col commanding. Any violation of this order will be followed by the immediate seizure and destruction of all of the liquors of the offender, and by such other punishment as the nature of the case may demand. A vigilant patrol will be organized to visit suspected places wagons, rooms, booths, etc., and to carry these orders into execution.

J.K. ARNOLD
Adjutant 7th Reg't Min. Vols.
Post Adjutant

    The same military that had ended the savagery and captured the aggressors had now committed to protect them even from its own members. Later orders would deny the sale of intoxicants to the general population, and martial law further restrict their behavior. Threats of vigilante justice, verbal or published, were taken seriously. But the President had ruled, and those orders would be carried out.

    The gallows were constructed on the bank of the Minnesota River across from the stone jail, where its progress might be seen by those who were to hang from it. Built in a 24-ft. square of heavy white oak timbers, about 20 ft. in height, its scaffold supported 40 hangman's ropes, ten on each side. The platform on all sides was connected to a single rope, and had been tested time and again to make certain that it operated properly. The construction process itself drew crowds of hundreds. The hangings were to be an act of justice, but they also reeked of unmitigated revenge, and those who had suffered losses in the carnage were determined to milk the process for every last bit of it.

December 22, 1862

At 2:30 in the afternoon on this overcast Monday, the 39 prisoners were gathered into the only room in the jail big enough to hold all of them, for the purpose of having their death sentence read. With many of the condemned seated on the floor, and most expressionless, Reverend Mr. Riggs interpreted Col. Miller's words:

The commanding officer at this place has called to speak to you upon a very serious subject this afternoon. Your Great Father at Washington, after carefully reviewing what the witnesses have testified in your several trials, has come to the conclusion that you have each been guilty of wantonly and wickedly murdering his white children; and for this reason he has directed that you each be hanged by the neck until dead, on next Friday; and that order will be carried into effect on that day, at ten o'clock in the forenoon. Good ministers – both Catholic and Protestant – are here, from amongst whom each of you can select your spiritual advisor, who will be permitted to commune with you constantly during the four days you are yet to live.

Following the reading, meetings between the prisoners and their selected spiritual advisors were arranged, more kinikinic tobacco was produced for those who smoked, and the condemned moved to another room in the stone building, chained two by two, and placed under heavy guard.

December 24, 1862
Headquarters Indian Post
Mankato
GENERAL ORDER NO. 21
    The Colonel Commanding publishes the following Rules to Govern all who may be concerned; and for the preservation of the public peace declares Martial Law over all the territory within a circle of ten miles of these headquarters.
                              STEPHEN MILLER
                              Col. 7th Reg't Min. Vols.
                              Commanding Post

December 25, 1862
    A special order from the President is received by Col. Miller, postponing the execution of one of the prisoners, Ta-ti-mi-na, reducing the number to be hung to 38.

December 26, 1862
    It was, according to one witness, "a beautiful day for a hanging". The temperature approached 50 degrees under a cloudless sky, and many of the assembled witnesses attended in shirtsleeves. Overall, it was a bitterly carnival atmosphere, most of the spectators projecting grim expressions, fists unconsciously clenched, others with tears running down their cheeks. While what was to happen would serve to satisfy their own carnal instincts, it would not bring back the slain,

nor the tortured minds of the maimed and the witnesses to unspeakable horror.

Over 5,000 were estimated to be in attendance, "packing every inch of available space in the streets", even filling the massive sandbar in the middle of the river.

The crowds were separated from the gallows by a human phalanx of soldiers from the 6th, 7th, 9th, and 10th regiments, Captain White's mounted men, and the 1st Regiment's Mounted Rangers. In all, 1,419 troopers and over 300 horses stood between the condemned and the angry crowd. An estimated 200 physicians and "medical men" were in attendance as well, hoping to acquire at least one of the cadavers for medical research.

Standing inside the square, already fingering a newly-sharpened axe, stood Captain John Duly, who had asked for the job of executioner. Three of his children had been killed by the rampaging Indians, and his wife and two other children were still captives of Little Crow.

During the previous days, the prisoners had been consoled by Father Ravoux, a Catholic priest, and the Rev. T.S. Williamson, who was both a physician and Protestant missionary. All but two had been baptized into the Christian faith.

This day, at 7:30 in the morning, the shackles and chains were removed from the prisoners, and their arms tied in front of them. Most were silent, though as the moments passed a sense of almost cheerful resignation passed among them, and many awkwardly shook hands with the soldiers, said goodbye to them, and conversed with their fellow prisoners, seemingly relieved that the process was about to be over. Some were painted; most wore shawls or blankets over their shoulders. All wore prominently-displayed religious symbols.

Just before 10:00, Father Ravoux read a prayer to the group, and spoke to them of their heavenly father. The priest had taken his role as spiritual mentor seriously, and was respected by most of the Indians. His sincere last words brought tears to the eyes of many of them.

While he was speaking, Captain G.D.Redfield, provost marshall, entered the room and announced that all was ready. Immediately, all were on their feet and moving hastily through the door, as if to demonstrate their courage by being first to climb the scaffold.

Once outside, and in full view of the imposing gallows, the fourteen-hundred uniformed soldiers and 5000 grim-faced spectators, the condemned broke into their death chant, an eerie, wailing acknowledgement of the fate that was before them. They were led by guard reliefs, unarmed, between two files of soldiers marking the path to their destination. Eight men were detailed to the scaffold, two to each section of the platform, to act as official executioners. Two troopers with axes were prepared for any emergency. While the executioners pulled muslin hoods over their eyes, and adjusted the nooses around their necks, the condemned continued their death chant, swaying back and forth, and crying out "I am here, I am here".

The Indians' "mournful wails" were interrupted by occasional screams. Several of the marauders turned, in pitiful attempts to hold the hands of their hooded neighbor. Two of the younger braves cried, shoulders shaking.

At 10:16, Major Brown, standing just beyond the stair to the scaffold, signaled to Captain Duly, shirt stained with perspiration, to approach the rope tautly-secured in the center of the gallows. Then, raising his sticks to signal silence, the Major slowly, almost theatrically, lowered them and beat three distinct taps on his drum. At the third tap, William Duly, himself now sobbing with emotion, raised his axe – and missed the rope. He looked quickly at Major Brown, who was continuing a soft roll and simply nodded at the nervous executioner. Captain Duly once again raised his axe, paused, and brought it down with a cry and a resounding thud. The platform on all four sides fell away and the chant was abruptly silenced as 37 Sioux warriors hung by their necks, most writhing but momentarily before hanging still. A few "kicked savagely". One, a heavy man, broke the rope, and fell to the ground. Though with a broken neck, he was immediately carried back to the platform to be hung a second time.

The roar that broke from the surrounding crowd at this last hanging was so demanding, so visceral that the troops surrounding the gallows were ordered to "about face" to keep the throng from breaking through seeking macabre souvenirs. The mounted troopers had an especially difficult time keeping their horses under control during the uproar, which was several minutes in length.

Drs. Seignorette and Finch were recruited to examine the bodies, and after a period of less than half an hour reported to the officer of the day that all were dead. Within minutes, all had been cut down, loaded into the four wagons acquired for the purpose, and taken for burial to a long trench dug out near the riverbank. Once again, the Indians were subjected on the way to the wrath of the populace, in spite of the escort provided by mounted troopers. It was a desecration eagerly adopted by onlookers.

During the afternoon, a group of soldiers out of uniform tied one of the cadavers to a tree, using it for target practice. Later, a physician was seen leaving town with a dead Indian tied erect behind him. The following morning, a group of young boys seeking "keepsakes" from the bodies were disappointed to find the grave opened, and empty.

CHAPTER FORTY THREE

July 3, 1863

Over six months had passed since the hangings at Mankato, but the populace felt no more secure. The Indians were still raiding, and Little Crow himself had managed to avoid capture, his whereabouts unknown. Most of the settlers from the village of Hutchinson had arranged housing near the stockade, only venturing forth to attend their fields in the company of others, and well armed. Birney Lamson had walked to the village to spend the July 4 holiday. His brother Chauncey and father Nathan had gone to the family farm 6 miles north of the village, and on that evening had decided to go deer hunting. An hour before sundown they were a good two miles northwest of the farm, walking along a road running through a marsh. Suddenly they saw an Indian jumping on his horse just beyond a large blackberry patch, and strike off toward the west. Thankfully, they were not seen, because, according to Birney, "....to see an Indian meant death to him or his white enemy in those days".

Nathan was a true frontiersman, sixty-three years old, tough, and wise in the ways of the frontier. Chauncey was an adept student. The two had noted at least two Indians, but were unsure of how many more might be lurking in the patch. After a discussion, Chauncey took a position covering the road between them and the patch, while Nathan took to the bushes leading to the patch and began creeping forward. Both had single-shot rifles.

Ten days earlier, Little Crow had left his hideaway in Dakota Territory, determined to wreak some sort of personal revenge on the settlers who had so thoroughly humiliated him and punctured any possibility of progress for his nation. He brought with him a small band consisting of his son Wo-wi-napa (One who appeareth), Hi-u-ka, a son-in-law, and four others. They had already conducted a number of raids, including the murder of James McGannon in nearby Wright County. Now they were after horses, and something to eat.

    Nathan lined up behind a poplar tree which stood directly between him and the Indians, and edged toward it on his stomach. On reaching the tree, which was covered with a coating of vines, he stood and was able to sight two remaining Indians. From a distance of no more than 35 feet he shot the larger of the two, the ball entering the left groin. Both Indians and Nathan went to ground after the shot, neither being able to locate the other. For a minute all was silent. Chauncey couldn't see to get a shot off, and Nathan had a pistol, but was unfamiliar with it, and decided to hold off unless he and the enemy came face to face. Still behind the tree, and frantically trying to reload, Nathan noticed the black-powder smoke from his first shot now rising in front of the tree, knew it would be seen by the Indians, and ran back in its line just as a single slug and a dozen buckshot pellets lodged in it. Ducking now in the bushes between the tree and the road, he tried once again to reload his rifle, only to find that the balls he had were too large for the bore, and lodged a finger's length down from the muzzle.

    Worried now, he removed his white shirt in an attempt at some sort of camouflage, hurriedly crossed the road where his son still provided cover, and hid behind a clump of hazel brush about 16 ft. across, determined to stay until discovered and then use his pistol.

    Little Crow skulked around the perimeter of the blackberry patch and came down the bushes alongside the road, projecting a double-barreled shotgun in front of him almost like a spear, and heading toward the hazel brush concealing Nathan. When the wounded Indian got in range, Chauncey stood up and confronted him, both men immobile for a split second, then firing virtually simultaneously, the shotgun's roar drowning out the crack of Chauncey' rifle. A slug from Little Crow's shotgun grazed the young man's head; Chauncey's bullet struck the stock of Little Crow's weapon and entered his left breast, stopping just inside the skin of his back. Both men went down.

Chauncey attempted to re-load his rifle, only to discover that he had no bullets. After several minutes, unarmed and not knowing the whereabouts of his dad, he sought to draw the Indians away from his father, and stood up in the center of the bush and began running for the village some 8 miles down the road.

Nathan, slightly grazed by buckshot, lay still in the thick brush no more than 15 feet from where Little Crow had fallen. In moments, a younger Indian called out to Little Crow, then stealthfully approached and lay down with the older one. For an hour, Nathan listened to the moans of the wounded man, and what he could understand of the conversation between them. Then silence. Then the younger man's pleading, a shaking of the older man, then silence. Another ten minutes, and the boy rose, looked carefully around, and trotted off to where a second pony had been hidden.

When he was barely out of sight, Nathan hefted his pistol and ventured a kneeling observation of the spot where the older man lay. After determining that he was dead, Nathan arose and walked steadily into the village, pistol in his right hand. He reached town at 4:00 in the morning; Chauncey had arrived at 10:00 the previous evening, and had assembled a party of thirteen soldiers and five civilians, returning first to the family's homestead, then to the scene of the shooting. Finding the body of the older Indian and determining to leave it for the moment, the party began to pursue the trail of the pony they'd seen initially, only to pass that task on to a small cavalry patrol they soon encountered.

While they'd been gone, Nathan had returned with a wagon and a neighbor to carry the body into town, only to find that the corpse had been scalped by a member of the cavalry patrol to get, Nathan guessed, the bounty offered by the state.

Nathan and his neighbor were greeted by jubilant townsfolk upon their arrival this 4th of July with another good/dead Indian. But their joy turned into unabashed hysteria when Private Hiram Cummins, Company E, Ninth Minnesota Volunteers, pointed out the double row of teeth and the two broken and badly re-set wrists that served as the "fingerprints" of Little Crow, the perpetrator of the most massive single massacre in the history of the United States.

The body of Taoyateduta, the Little Crow, third in a dynasty of Dakota leaders and one-time guest of the Great Father, the President of the United States, was displayed briefly, used as a target for missiles of various forms, then tossed among the garbage in the town dump before being recovered that same day, and savagely beheaded - the signal final chapter in the Great Sioux Uprising of 1862.

A week later, both the fact and the form of his demise was a message received with enthusiasm by *Captain* Timothy J. Sheehan, at that moment busily engaged in the more *civilized* brutality between whites that helped to spark those historic and mind-numbing events that, in the heat of his current battles, seemed so long ago.

Made in the USA
Charleston, SC
31 December 2011